TABLE OF CONTENTS

"I am the light of the world. He who follows Me shall not walk in darkness, but have the light of life." (John 8:12)

A Dynamic Soul-winning Manual to Lead Your Church Into a Powerful Bible Study Ministry

By Ernestine & Mark Finley

PUBLISHED BY HART BOOKS
A MINISTRY OF HART RESEARCH CENTER

By Ernestine & Mark Finley

PUBLISHED BY HART BOOKS
A MINISTRY OF HART RESEARCH CENTER
Contact Hart Research Center at: 1-800-487-4278
or visit us on the web at: www.hartresearch.org
visit *It Is Written* online at: www.iiw.org

Design: Fred Knopper, Linda Anderson McDonald
Editing: Judy Knopper, Michele Stotz
Type set: 13/16 Clearface
Printed in the United States of America,

The authors assume responsibility for the accuracy of all facts and quotations as cited in this book. All quotation emphasis supplied by the authors.

ISBN: 1-878046-60-8

INTRODUCTION

Tens of thousands of Seventh-day Adventist lay people worldwide are rediscovering the joy of sharing their faith. They have a new understanding of their role as Christians. The Biblical truth of God's call to be His witnesses has lifted their vision and transformed their lives. They are sharing their faith with renewed enthusiasm. A sense of excitement about what God is doing through them has elevated their own spiritual experience to new heights.

Where the church is growing around the world, lay people are actively involved. Evangelistic success is largely dependent on an active laity.

Lay people, distributing literature, sharing Christ with their friends, visiting their neighbors and giving Bible studies, **are making a dramatic difference in the advancement of God's kingdom.**

These consecrated lay people are participating in the largest evangelistic thrust in history. They are seeing scores accept God's truth for this hour. Over 2,800 people every single day—or one million per year—are becoming Seventh-day Adventists. Most of these new converts can trace their conversion to the loving witness of a church member.

Adventist lay people realize that we are living on the verge of the kingdom of God. They have a growing conviction that the coming of our Lord is near. **Church members are giving their time, using their gifts and actively witnessing for their Lord.**

Two thousand years ago, **Jesus gave a clarion call to service** to the New Testament church. His words are too plain to be misunderstood:

> "**Go** therefore, and **make** disciples of all the nations, **baptizing** them in the name of the Father and of the Son and of the Holy Spirit, teaching them to observe all things that I have commanded you; and lo, I am with you always, even to the end of the age."
>
> *MATTHEW 28:19-20*

Ellen White, God's last-day messenger, clearly describes how the work of the great gospel commission can be accomplished.

> "This can best be done by **personal efforts**, by bringing the truth into their houses, praying with them, and opening to them the Scriptures."
>
> *REVIEW AND HERALD*, DECEMBER 8, 1885

> "It is the privilege of every Christian not only to look for but to **hasten the coming of our Lord Jesus Christ**."
>
> *CHRIST'S OBJECT LESSONS*, PAGE 69

> "Long has God waited for the **spirit of service** to take possession of the whole church, so that every one shall be working for Him according to his ability."
>
> *ACTS OF THE APOSTLES*, PAGE 111

Lay involvement is the key to fulfilling the great gospel commission. Listen to this inspired statement:

> "**The work of God in this earth can never be finished until** the men and women comprising our church membership rally to the work and unite their efforts with those of ministers and church officers."
>
> *GOSPEL WORKERS*, PAGE 352

God is gathering lay people around the world for a final movement at the climax of earth's history. He will pour out His Spirit on them as they use their gifts to proclaim the Good News.

Evangelism is the dynamic heartbeat of the New Testament church. The book of **Acts is alive with lay people witnessing for their Lord**. Jesus called Peter, a fisherman, Matthew, a tax collector, and Luke, a physician, to be His witnesses. Lay people, both men and women, were called to share their faith. On the day of Pentecost, 3,000 were baptized in a day.

A few months later, the church grew to 5,000 men, not even counting women and children. The Christian church numbered from between 15,000 to 20,000 shortly after Pentecost.

What caused this unprecedented evangelistic explosion? **The entire church was focused on the central objective of winning the lost to Christ**. Each member had a passion for soul-winning. Their energies were directed to saving lost people.

The book of Acts is being repeated today. Once again, lay people are becoming enthusiastic about sharing their faith. Once again, there is a new openness in society and thousands are being baptized. Christians now know what work they have to do.

> "Our work has been marked out for us by our Heavenly Father. We are to **take our Bibles, and go forth to warn the world**. We are to be God's helping hands in saving souls—channels through which His love is day-by-day to flow to the perishing."
>
> *TESTIMONIES,* VOLUME 9, PAGE 150

This manual will take you through the simple, practical steps of becoming actively involved in many different ministries, but particularly by sharing God's word through Bible study ministry. Although there are many ways of sharing our faith, God has especially called upon some to open His word and share His truth with others. As you apply the principles of this manual to your life, you will be enormously blessed. Your church will grow and God's Kingdom will be advanced. **So let's begin.**

CHAPTER 1

FIVE KEYS TO SUCCESSFUL EVANGELISM

A Master Strategy Based on Five Church Growth Principles

The "Five Keys To Successful Evangelism" are Biblical, Christ-centered principles that testify to their explosive power by producing growing churches.

A careful study of the book of Acts reveals the disciples' success was based on these five **universal principles**. These eternal evangelistic principles **bridge cultural barriers** and ensure success in soul-winning. They have been **field-tested** around the world. By understanding these "Five Keys," pastors and lay people have become more successful in winning lost souls to Christ. As **these principles** are implemented in local congregations, the Holy Spirit works powerfully to **produce unusual growth for the kingdom of God**.

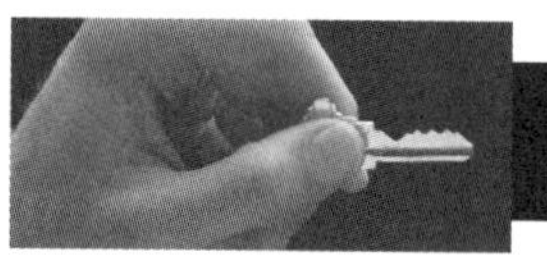

KEY 1 • REVIVAL

Churches grow when there is a genuine **spiritual revival** among the members and a corresponding renewal of spiritual life.

The New Testament Christian church grew largely because each member experienced a personal encounter with Jesus Christ. The book of Acts testifies to the dynamic power of God working through converted believers. Notice how these clear passages reveal Christ's promise of spiritual revival and its dramatic effect on the lives of the disciples:

> Acts 1:8 – "But **you shall receive power** when the Holy Spirit has come upon you and you shall be witnesses unto me."

Acts 4:20 – "For we cannot but speak the things **we have seen and heard**." (The testimony of the disciples was from the depths of their personal experiences.)

Acts 4:31 – "When **they prayed** the place was shaken; and they were **all filled with the Holy Spirit**, and **they spoke the word of God with boldness**."

Acts 4:33 – "And **with great power** the disciples gave witness of the resurrection."

The Apostle John describes these spirit-filled disciples and the power of their witness this way,

> "That which was from the beginning, which **we have heard**, which we **have seen with our eyes**, which **we have looked upon** and **our hands have handled** concerning the word of life, the life was manifested and **we have seen** and **bear witness** and **declare to you that eternal life** which was with the Father and was manifested to us—that which we have **seen and heard we declare to you**, that you also may have fellowship with us; and truly our fellowship is with the Father and with His Son Jesus Christ."
>
> *I JOHN 1:1-3*

- The disciples shared a Christ they knew.
- They proclaimed a Christ whom they experienced.
- They witnessed of a Christ who changed them personally.

On the Day of Pentecost the disciples experienced spiritual revival. (See Acts 2:1-4)

The newly-converted disciples, filled with the Spirit, had hearts overflowing with the desire to proclaim His love to everyone they met. When we have an experience with Jesus, we too will have a desire to share Him.

> "No sooner does one come to Christ than there is **born in his heart a desire to make known to others what a precious friend he has found in Jesus**, the saving and sanctifying truth cannot be shut up in his heart."
>
> *STEPS TO CHRIST*, PAGE 78

There is a great need for revival among God's people. God longs to give us His Holy Spirit. He is waiting for us to accept it.

"A revival of true godliness among us is the greatest and most urgent of all our needs. To seek this should be our first work. There must be earnest effort to obtain the blessing of the Lord, not because God is not willing to bestow His blessing upon us, but because we are unprepared to receive it. **Our heavenly Father is more willing to give His Holy Spirit to them that ask Him, then are earthly parents to give good gifts to their children.**"

1 SELECTED MESSAGES, PAGE 121

THREE WAYS WE CAN EXPERIENCE A SPIRITUAL REVIVAL

Churches are revived when there is a renewed emphasis on ***Bible study.***

"Grace and peace be multiplied to you in the knowledge of God and of Jesus our Lord, as His divine power has given to us all things that pertain to life and godliness, through the knowledge of Him who called us by glory and virtue, by which have been given to us exceedingly **great and precious promises**, that **through these you may be partakers of the divine nature**, having escaped the corruption that is in the world through lust."

II PETER 1:2-4

"There **is nothing more calculated to strengthen the intellect than the study of the Scriptures**. No other book is so potent to elevate the thoughts, to give vigor to the faculties, as the broad, ennobling truths of the Bible."

STEPS TO CHRIST, PAGE 90

"Let us **give more time to the study of the Bible**. We do not understand the word as we should. The book of Revelation opens with an injunction to us to understand the instruction that it contains. 'Blessed is he that readeth, and they that hear the words of this prophecy,' God declares, 'and keep those things which are written therein: for the time is at hand.' When we as a people understand what this book means to us, there will be seen among us a great revival."

TESTIMONIES, TO MINISTERS, PAGE 113

Churches are revived when there is a renewed emphasis on ***intercessory prayer.***

Paul prayed for the saints and faithful brethren in Christ who were in Colosse. You can see Paul's example of intercession in Colossians 1:3, 9 and Philippians 1:3-5.

> "We give thanks to the God and Father of our Lord Jesus Christ, **praying always** for you... For this reason we also, since the day we heard it, **do not cease to pray for you**, and to ask that you may be filled with the knowledge of His will in all wisdom and spiritual understanding."
>
> *COLOSSIANS 1:3, 9*

> "I thank my God upon every remembrance of you, **always in every prayer** of mine **making request for you** all with joy, for your fellowship in the gospel from the first day until now."
>
> *PHILIPPIANS 1:3-5*

> "There is necessity for diligence in prayer; let nothing hinder you. Make every effort to keep open the communion between Jesus and your own soul."
>
> *STEPS TO CHRIST*, PAGE 98

Churches are revived when there is a renewed emphasis on ***witnessing.***

As the disciples shared their faith, it grew. As they testified of their personal commitment to Christ, they became powerful proclaimers. The more we give, the more we will receive.

> "If you will go to work as Christ designs that His disciples shall, and win souls for Him, you will feel the need of a deeper experience and a greater knowledge in divine things, and will hunger and thirst after righteousness."
>
> *STEPS TO CHRIST*, PAGE 80

In your own words, please summarize the essential principles of revival in a local congregation.

____

____

____

After a person has spent time with Jesus and is spiritually renewed, the heart's desire is to be trained and equipped for service.

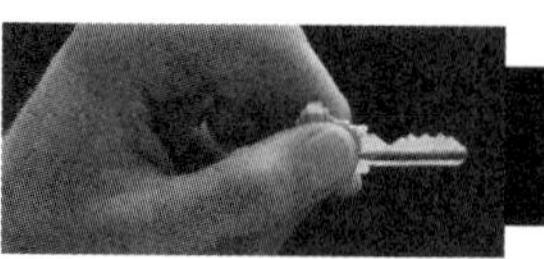

KEY 2 • EQUIPPING

Churches grow when each member is **trained and equipped** for service.

Our Lord encouraged the disciples to follow Him with these words: "Follow Me and I will make you fishers of men." (Matthew 4:19)

The disciples were equipped and trained by the world's greatest teacher. Jesus spent three and a half years training and equipping His disciples. In the book of Acts, they applied the lessons Jesus taught them. The disciples went out in Jesus' name, meeting the needs of men and women touching them for the kingdom of God.

As they **participated** in this **"hands-on" training** program with both **personal instruction** and **practical field experience**, they gradually **became** the **effective witnesses** Christ could use to turn the world upside down.

The Apostle Paul encouraged every pastor to equip the believers for the work of ministry.

> "And He Himself gave some to be apostles, some prophets, some evangelists, and some pastors, and teachers, **for the equipping of the saints for the work of ministry**, for the edifying of the body of Christ."
>
> *EPHESIANS 4:11-12*

> "**Many would be willing to work if they were taught how to begin**. They need to be instructed and encouraged. Every church should be a training school for Christian workers. Its members should be taught how to give Bible readings, how to conduct and teach Sabbath School classes, how best to help the poor and to care for the sick, and how to work for the unconverted. There should be schools of health, cooking schools and classes in various lines of Christian help work. There should not only be teaching, but actual work under experienced instructors. Let the teachers lead the way in working among the people, and others, uniting with them, will learn from their example. One example is worth more than many precepts."
>
> *MINISTRY OF HEALING*, PAGE 149

A worker who has been trained and equipped for the work can accomplish far more than workers who have not been trained.

> "**One worker** who has been **trained and educated for the work**, who is controlled by the Spirit of Christ, **will accomplish far more than ten laborers** who go out deficient in knowledge and weak in the faith."
>
> *EVANGELISM*, PAGE 474

If every church member should be engaged in some line of service for the Master, where do we begin? Ellen White tells us in the book *Evangelism*.

> "In our churches **let companies be formed for service**. The formation of small companies as a basis of Christian effort is a plan that has been presented before me by One who cannot err."
>
> *EVANGELISM*, PAGE 115

When church members are equipped to serve, and as they form small groups to reach out to their community in **Bible-based ministries**, the church will explode in growth.

A **revived church**, filled with members and equipped to witness, is a church that is ready to reach its community.

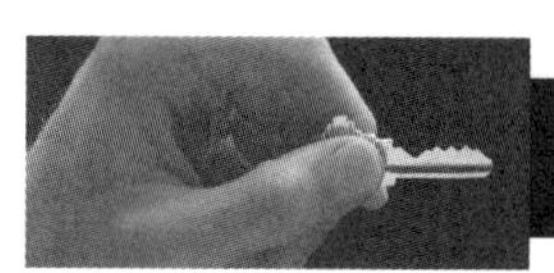

KEY 3 • COMMUNITY OUTREACH

Churches grow when there is a planned process of **community outreach** meeting the physical, mental, social and spiritual needs of people.

Jesus' ministry was people-focused. He met the needs of men and women. He was concerned about them.

> "Now Jesus went about all Galilee, **teaching** in their synagogues, **preaching** the gospel of the kingdom, and **healing** all kinds of sickness and all kinds of disease among the people."
>
> *MATTHEW 4:23*

He lovingly met their felt-needs. As their hearts opened, He shared the eternal principles of the kingdom with them.

Following the Savior's example, the New Testament church met the needs of people in Jesus' name. These early disciples demonstrated a concern for the entire person: physically, mentally, socially and spiritually. (See Acts 3:6, Acts 6:1-4)

> "**Christ's method alone will give true success in reaching the people.** The Savior mingled with men as one who desired their good. He showed His sympathy for them, ministered to their needs, and won their confidence. Then He bade them, 'Follow Me.'"
>
> *MINISTRY OF HEALING*, PAGE 143

Growing churches have a variety of programs that meet the needs of varied people groups. Just as Jesus met the physical, mental, emotional and spiritual needs, His people, filled with His love, do the same.

> "**Medical missionary work gives opportunity for carrying forward successful evangelistic work.** It is as these lines of effort are united, that we may expect to gather the most precious fruit for the Lord."
>
> *EVANGELISM*, PAGE 516

In both the natural and spiritual world there are laws of the harvest. One of the most basic is simply this, "**If you want to have a harvest it is necessary to sow the seed.**" No farmer expects God to work a miracle and germinate seed that he has not sown.

The only **visits** God can bless are the ones **we make**. The only **literature** God can bless is literature **we distribute**. The only **prayers** God can bless for souls are prayers **we offer**. The only **Bible studies** God can bless are the ones **we give**. The only **evangelistic seminars** God can bless are the ones **we conduct**. It is presumptuous to believe we can have a great harvest without adequate effort in sowing the seed of God's word. In fact, it is in the process of sowing that our own hearts are watered by the Holy Spirit and prepared for the harvest. As we participate with Christ in touching the lives of others with the gospel, the Holy Spirit transforms our own heart making our churches centers of His healing grace.

When interest in the gospel is developed through Bible studies and felt-need ministries, the fourth key logically follows.

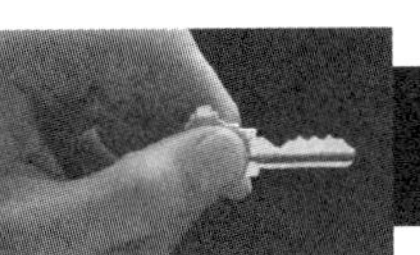

KEY 4 • REAPING

Churches grow when God's word is preached through evangelistic proclamation. Evangelistic churches are growing churches.

The New Testament Church placed priority on evangelism. They confidently shared God's word anticipating the Spirit's blessing.

Acts 4:31 – "They **spoke** the **word** of God with boldness."

Acts 5:42 – "And daily in the temple, and in every house, they **did not cease teaching and preaching Jesus as the Christ**."

Acts 8:4 – "Therefore those who were scattered **went everywhere preaching the word**."

When the **gospel seed has been sown**, it is **time to reap** a harvest. **God promises** to grant **a harvest** through biblical preaching and public evangelism. The disciples were powerful evangelists. Thousands responded to the sermons of Peter and Paul. Luke describes the growth of the church this way in:

Acts 6:7 – "And the **word of God spread** and the **number of disciples grew greatly**."

The preached word transforms lives. Evangelistic preaching changes lives.

> "Most startling messages will be borne by men of God's appointment, messages of a character to warn the people, to arouse them... **We must also have, in our cities, consecrated evangelists through whom a message is to be born so decidedly as to startle the hearers.**"
>
> *EVANGELISM*, PAGE 168

Around the world today, pastors, administrators and lay people are accepting the challenge and seizing the opportunity to share Christ's truth in public evangelism. There is a renewed interest on the part of lay people in preaching the word themselves. They have sensed God's call. Utilizing the many resources available they are proclaiming God's word with power.

The **fifth key** was a significant part of the disciples' evangelistic strategy. When people accepted Christ, understood His word and were baptized, they were integrated into a nurturing body of believers. The book of Acts describes their experience in these words:

> "And they **continued steadfastly** in the apostles' doctrine and fellowship, in the breaking of bread, and in prayers."
>
> *ACTS 2:42*

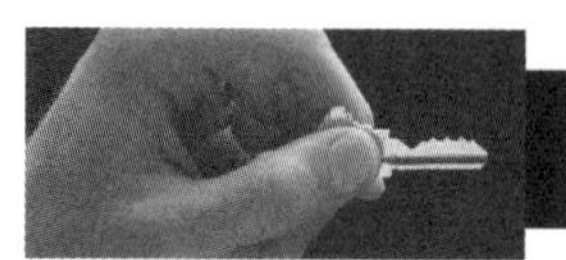

KEY 5 • NURTURE AND FOLLOW-UP

Churches grow when new converts are **nurtured** and taught to witness.

Growing churches nurture their new believers. Follow-up of the interest generated by public evangelism is an ongoing part of the church's effective outreach.

> "When men and women **accept the truth**, we are not to go away and leave them and have no further burden for them. They are **to be looked after.**"
>
> *EVANGELISM*, PAGE 345

We do not **dip them** and **drop them**. We **immerse them** and **instruct them**.

Jesus said to Peter, "When you are converted, strengthen your brethren." He also asked Peter, "Do you love Me?" Then said, "Feed My lambs."

Our love for Jesus leads us to a deep concern about the spiritual growth of new believers. As new believers develop their own prayer life, a personal devotional life through Bible study and become actively involved in witnessing, they will continue to grow spiritually. One of the most effective methods of helping new believers grow in Christ is to teach them how to share their faith.

> "**After individuals have been converted to the truth**, they need to be **looked after**...these newly converted ones **need nursing, watchful attention, help** and **encouragement**. These should **not be left alone**, a prey to Satan's most powerful temptation; they need to be **educated** in regard to their duties, to be **kindly dealt with** to be **led along**, and to be **visited and prayed with**..."
>
> *EVANGELISM*, PAGE 351 AND *GOSPEL WORKERS*, PAGE 322

Let's identify the principles that will anchor new believers in their faith:

- New believers grow in faith when they develop a meaningful devotional life.
- New believers grow when they are equipped to serve.
- New believers grow when they get involved in ministering to others.
- New believers grow when they become actively involved in sharing the word of God with others.
- New believers grow when they develop a friendship network with the church.

When Jesus met Nicodemus in a secluded night meeting, the Savior shocked the Pharisee by declaring, "You must be born again." Just as spiritually-complacent individuals need to be reborn, so entire congregations need a rebirth of evangelistic vision.

ENTIRE CONGREGATIONS
NEED A REBIRTH.

Churches are R-E-B-O-R-N when they teach, follow and implement:

KEY 1 **REVIVAL** **strategies of prayer, Bible study and witness**

KEY 2 **EQUIPPING** **church members to reach the community through Bible-based ministries**

KEY 3 **OUTREACH** **programs in the community**

KEY 4 **REAPING** **through evangelistic meetings**

KEY 5 **NURTURING** **events for the new believers**

As you carefully study each lesson in this manual you will discover how to **implement** each of these **explosive church-growth principles** and your church will be radically **REBORN**.

Evangelistic Countdown Calendar

A good place to begin is with "the plans." A builder always consults architectural drawings when building a house. In the same manner, effective soul-winning leaders must develop a master plan to build up the house of God. This master plan, placed in a calendar format, serves as the base of the entire soul-winning evangelistic program by outlining specific activities.

Preparing an evangelistic calendar is crucial. It is not possible to be effective in evangelism without detailed plans. This countdown calendar should include the "Five Keys to Successful Evangelism." These "Five Keys" are the foundation. Once you have the plans and the foundation, you are ready to build. The following is a sample 18-month calendar utilizing the "Five Keys to Successful Evangelism."

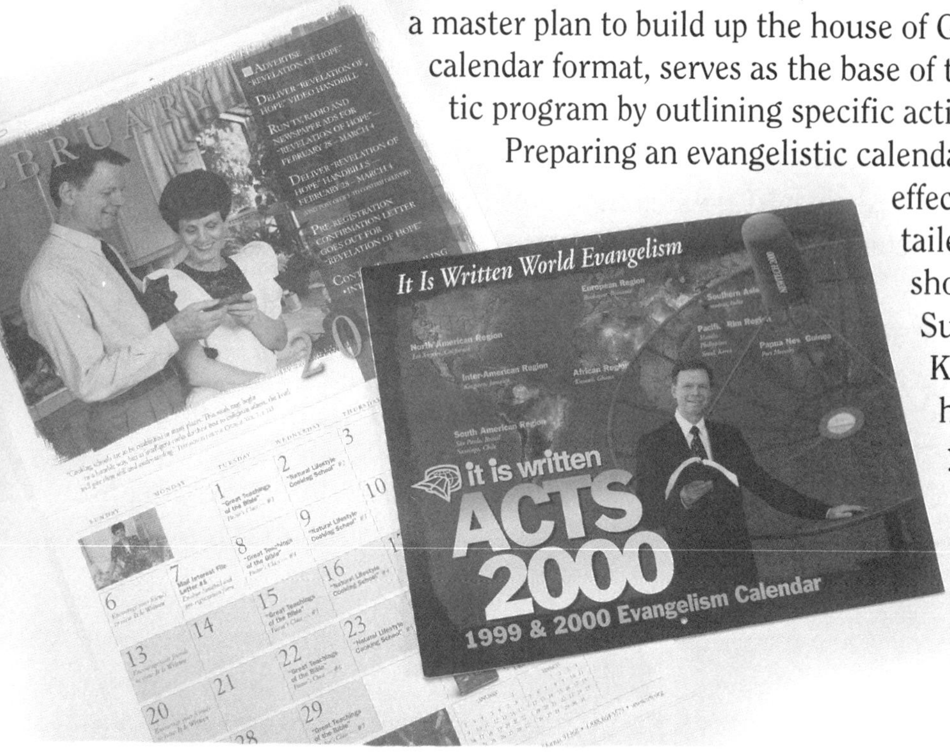

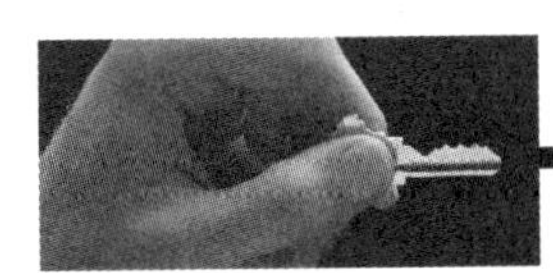

KEY 1 • REVIVAL

JANUARY – APRIL = 14 WEEKS

• Conduct *Fulfilling the Gospel Commission* (nine sessions) and *Making Friends For God* (five sessions). If your church has not gone through these seminars, it would be good to start with these 14 sessions.

• Study the Bible book of Acts—and review the evangelistic explosion that took place.

• Hold a revival weekend using the sermon series found in the book *The Final Days* (a series of sermons by Mark Finley available for purchase at 1-888-664-5573.)

KEY 2 • EQUIPPING

MAY – AUGUST = 16 WEEKS

• Use the *Light Your World For God* Bible study ministry manual.

• Cover two chapters an evening from, 7:00-9:00 p.m., over the next four weeks.

• After Chapter 8, "Developing Your Notebook and File Box," begin using the principles learned by going out into the field to find interests.

• Over the next 12 weeks, complete *Search for Certainty* Bible lessons and prepare file boxes.

• Lay Bible instructors should practice giving Bible studies to friends, neighbors, relatives or someone from the pastor's interest list.

• After approximately 16 weeks, organized training classes resume for the class on *Soup & Salvation.* During *Soup & Salvation*, trained lay members should begin taking other church members on Bible studies with them.

NOTE: Equipping and outreach activities will overlap. After the first four weeks of equipping and training, soul-winners should begin reaching out into the community to find interests.

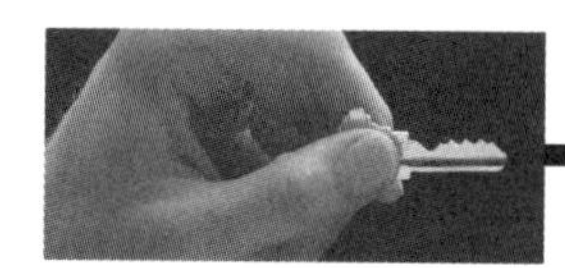

KEY 3 • OUTREACH

SEPTEMBER – JANUARY = 20 WEEKS

Bible-based ministries in the community

Although there are many community outreach programs that will produce interests for the evangelistic meetings, we have found the following to be most effective:

1. Bible studies
2. Home Bible seminars
3. Health expos and cooking schools
4. Archeology seminars

During this third key, pastors and trained lay members should:

- Find and develop interests
- Initiate Bible studies
- Conduct *Soup & Salvation* ministry for approximately 12 weeks
- Launch home Bible seminars 12 weeks before the evangelistic meetings begin

OPTIONAL
- Generate interests for the upcoming meetings by presenting a community cooking school five weeks before the event. (An all-day health expo can also be held.)
- Feature archeology seminars or other community programs prior to the evangelistic meetings.

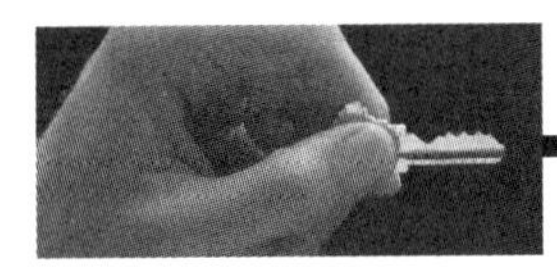

KEY 4 • REAPING

FEBRUARY – MARCH = SIX WEEKS (SEVEN WEEKENDS)

The most effective way to reap a harvest of souls is through public evangelistic meetings. Each series is usually conducted over five or six weeks depending on the series used. These meetings are presented by a "live" evangelist, or through the use of an evangelistic video series. (The *Discoveries in Prophecy* and *Revelation of Hope* evangelistic series are available through *It Is Written*.)

For preaching with a "live" evangelist use:

The *New Beginnings* DVD evangelistic series
The *Revelation of Hope* evangelistic computer graphics program

For preaching with the videos use:

Discoveries in Prophecy
Revelation of Hope
New Beginnings DVD Play-It version

KEY 5 • NURTURE AND FOLLOW-UP

APRIL – JULY = 18 WEEKS

When the "Five Keys to Successful Evangelism" are implemented in a church, God will bless with an abundant harvest of souls. During the last week of the evangelistic meetings, individuals will be baptized. They will be joining God's remnant church. It is critical that these new believers be nurtured. Therefore, during the last week of the evangelistic meetings, conduct a class on nurture and follow-up for the members of your local church. (See Chapter 14)

NOTES

CHAPTER 2

SOUL-WINNING A WISE CHOICE

Life is full of important choices. The direction our lives take is dependent upon the choices we make. We chart our course through life by our choices. Unfortunately, many people make choices only with reference to what brings them immediate pleasure. They then miss life's greatest joys by making superficial choices.

There are two significant choices that will impact our lives here and through all eternity.

CHOICE 1 • COMMITMENT TO GOD

The first and most serious choice is to commit our life to God. Jesus challenged people in His day to:

> "Seek first the kingdom of God and His righteousness..."
>
> *MATTHEW 6:33*

The priority that towers over all others is to make God first in our lives. The Old Testament spiritual giant Joshua stated it succinctly:

> "...Choose for yourselves this day whom you will serve...but as for me and my house, we will serve the Lord."
>
> *JOSHUA 24:15*

Augustine prayed,
"Lord our hearts will never find rest until they find rest in thee."

The choice to commit our life to God is the most important choice we will ever make. Closely allied to the choice to commit our life to God is the choice to live for God. God calls us to live a life of service. This choice speaks to the issue of our priorities. The things we consider important. This leads to the next most important choice.

CHOICE 2 • PRIORITIES

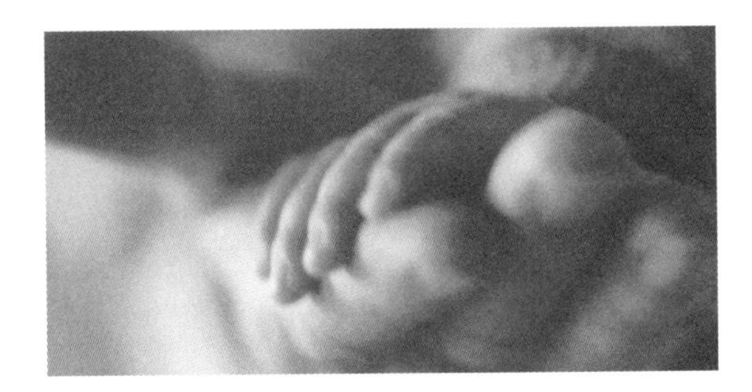

The second important choice has to do with our priorities.
Our priorities will:

- **Impact** our RELATIONSHIPS
- **Affect** our GOALS
- **Determine** how we spend our TIME
- **Influence** our ATTITUDES

The choice to place God's kingdom first will propel us to readjust our priorities in order to advance His kingdom.

Our commitment to Jesus and an understanding of His principle of seeking first the kingdom of God, leads us to re-evaluate how we spend our time. When our hearts are transformed by God's grace, the natural result is to share His love with others. We long to share the Christ we know. Our deepest desire is to lead others to a knowledge of eternal life. We long for them to be saved in God's kingdom. Our greatest satisfaction comes as others share in the joy Jesus has placed in our lives.

Question 1: What does the Bible reveal to be a wise choice? Proverbs 11:30 (last part)

Answer: ____

The most wonderful work in the world is soul-winning. The greatest call that any of us can have is the call to win someone to Jesus. They can then enjoy fellowship with God in this life, and have the joy of living with Him through all eternity.

Question 2: What promise has God given to those who make this wise choice to become soul-winners? Daniel 12:3

Answer: ____

Hollywood stars, sports stars and other stars come and go, but those who win souls will experience the results of their work forever. The results are eternal. People redeemed in the kingdom of God as a result of our cooperation with Christ will thank us through all eternity.

Someday you will meet someone in the earth made new who will say, **"Thank you, for sharing Jesus with me. I'm here because you prayed for me. You visited me. You studied the Bible with me."**

There is nothing more important we can do in our lives. Ellen White states it powerfully in these words:

> "**The greatest work**, the noblest effort, in which men [and women] can engage, is to **point sinners to the Lamb of God**."
>
> *GOSPEL WORKERS,* PAGE 18

Question 3: How does Jesus sum up the theme of His ministry? Luke 19:10

Answer: ______________________________

Jesus, the master soul-winner, placed the kingdom of God first in His own life. He placed priority on this one thing—the eternal salvation of men and women. Even at the cross He made one of life's wisest choices. **God's one-and-only Son was a soul-winner.** There is no higher calling than sharing God's love with others.

The message of salvation is the message of the entire Bible.

The Bible was written for two purposes:

- **To learn** how we can be saved.
- **To share** with others how they can be saved.

> "To save souls should be the life work of everyone who professes Christ. We are debtors to the world for the grace given us of God, for the light which has shone upon us, and for the discovered beauty and power of truth."
>
> *TESTIMONIES,* VOLUME 4, PAGE 53

William Carey, that great missionary to India, said, "I cobble shoes to pay expenses, but soul-winning is my business." William Carey's dedication is a powerful example for us. His life work was to win souls for Jesus. In the book *The Desire of Ages*, Ellen White echoes this same thought:

"The Spirit and the bride say, 'Come!' And let him that heareth say, 'Come!'" Rev. 22:17. Everyone who hears is to repeat the invitation. **Whatever one's calling in life, his first interest should be to win souls for Christ**...Christ would have His servant minister to sin-sick souls."

DESIRE OF AGES, PAGE 822

Question 4: What is the natural result of committing our lives to Christ? What happened when the demoniacs committed their lives to the Savior? Luke 8:35-39

Answer: ____

When the demoniacs consecrated themselves to Christ they immediately began sharing His love with others. They shared what Christ had done for them with their friends and neighbors. Here is an insightful comment by Ellen White from the book *Christian Service*.

> "The two restored demoniacs were the **first missionaries** whom Christ sent to preach the gospel in the region of Decapolis. For a few moments only, these men had been privileged to hear the teachings of Christ. Not one sermon from His lips had ever fallen upon their ears. They could not instruct the people as the disciples who had been daily with Christ were able to do. But they bore in their own persons the evidence that Jesus was the Messiah. They could tell what they knew, what they themselves had seen, and heard, and felt of the power of Christ. This is what everyone can do whose heart has been touched by the grace of God."
>
> *CHRISTIAN SERVICE*, PAGE 17

The only place to begin is where you are. **Ask the Lord to place a burden in your heart for one special person. Look for opportunities to share what Jesus has done for you. Open your heart and share how Christ has forgiven you and changed your own life.**

In this program, you will discover:

- How to use the gifts God has given you to become an effective soul-winner.
- How to effectively share Jesus with others.
- How to discover new Bible study interests.
- How to give Bible studies and lead people to a decision for Christ.

Soul-winning is much more than the art of sharing information. It is the art of reaching the heart. This can occur if we ourselves are totally consecrated to God.

> "It is only by a daily consecration to God that you can become soul-winners...God can work with those only who will accept the invitation: 'Come unto Me, all you that labor and are heavy-laden, and I will give you rest. Take my yoke upon you, and learn of Me; for I am meek and lowly in heart; and you shall find rest unto your souls. For My yoke is easy, and My burden is light.' *Matthew 11:28-30.*"
>
> *TESTIMONIES,* VOLUME 6, PAGE 318

We cannot effectively share a Jesus we don't know. We will have little impact on the lives of others if Christ has had little impact on our lives. **It is difficult to win someone else to Christ if we have not been won to Christ ourselves.**

If you have not fully surrendered your life to Christ why not begin this seminar by making that commitment right now? If you have already surrendered your life to Jesus, why not make a deeper commitment to Him than you have ever made before? Why not open your heart fully to Jesus? Why not ask Him to take away anything that will keep you from becoming the most effective soul-winner possible?

In these next few lessons you will discover practical steps that will help you become an effective soul-winner for Jesus. Why not pray this simple prayer right now? *"Lord, lay some soul upon my heart, and love that soul through me, And may I nobly do my part, to win that soul for thee."* Make the best and a wise choice in life: **BE A SOUL-WINNER!**

CHAPTER 3

THE POWER OF THE HOLY SPIRIT & INTERCESSORY PRAYER

The story is told of a woman who spent months saving to purchase a new refrigerator. She was extremely disappointed when she discovered it didn't work. The milk spoiled, the fruit rotted and the vegetables wilted. Although this was the first refrigerator she had ever owned, she knew something was desperately wrong. How could she invest so much in a product that was so seriously flawed? The poor lady called the company she purchased the refrigerator from to file a complaint. They sent an appliance repairman to her home. He was amazed when he discovered the refrigerator was not plugged in properly. The plug was loose. There was simply no power. The most important thing that refrigerator needed was power. It needed to be connected to the source of power.

There are **many Christians with a "loose connection."** If they are going to be effective soul-winners they need to be connected to the source of all power. **It is power they need—Holy Spirit power.**

Ellen White reveals that a revival of Holy Spirit power is our greatest need.

> "**A revival of true godliness among us is the greatest and most urgent of all our needs.** To seek this should be our first work. There must be earnest effort to obtain the blessing of the Lord, not because God is not willing to bestow His blessing upon us, but because we are unprepared to receive it. **Our heavenly Father is more willing to give His Holy Spirit to them that ask Him, than are earthly parents to give good gifts to their children.** But it is our work, by confession, humiliation, repentance and earnest prayer, to fulfill the conditions upon which God has promised to grant us His blessing."
>
> *I SELECTED MESSAGES*, PAGE 121

It is impossible to be a successful witness for God without the power of the Holy Spirit flowing into our lives. In this lesson we will discover how to receive the power of the Holy Spirit to become effective soul-winners. We shall also learn the art of life-changing intercessory prayer. *Let's begin.*

RECEIVING THE SPIRIT

The Bible outlines some practical steps we can take to prepare our hearts to receive the Holy Spirit. We might call them the **ABC's** for receiving the Holy Spirit.

Question 1: What is the first condition for receiving the gift of the Holy Spirit? Luke 11:13

Answer:____

God invites us to **"ask for the Spirit."** The reason we are to ask is not because God is reluctant to give His Spirit, but because we are unprepared to receive it. Our asking prepares our hearts to receive. Asking is the first step in the process of reception.

Question 2: After we ask God for the Holy Spirit what is the next essential step? Mark 11:24

Answer: ____

Belief is faith that God will deliver on His promises when we meet the conditions. Belief is trusting God to do just what He says He will do. The first two conditions for receiving the Holy Spirit are asking God for His gift and believing He will fulfill His word.

> "Ask, **believe** and receive. There is too much mocking the Lord, too much praying that is not praying and that wearies angels and displeases God, too many vain, unmeaning petitions. First we should feel needy, and then ask God for the very things we need, believing that He gives them to us, even while we ask; and then our faith will grow, all will be edified, the weak will be strengthened, and the discouraged and desponding made to look up and believe that God is a rewarder of all those who diligently seek Him."
>
> *EARLY WRITINGS*, PAGE 115

Question 3: What is the third step in receiving the gift of the Holy Spirit? Acts 3:19

Answer____

Repentance is one aspect of confession. In true confession, we lay our hearts bare before God, acknowledging our sins and expressing heart felt sorrow for them. Repentance has to do with a change of mind or heart. This soul-sorrow, this sadness because we have broken God's heart, opens our own hearts to be effective witnesses. Before Pentecost, the upper room was a place of genuine confession and repentance. Before Pentecost, **the disciples asked for the spirit. They believed God's promise, claimed it by faith and opened their hearts to receive the Spirit through genuine confession and repentance.**

> "There is great need of the Holy Spirit's influence in our midst. There must be an individual work done in the breaking of stubborn hearts. There needs to be deep heart-searching that will lead to **confession of sin**. Believers should at this time stand with softened, sanctified, broken hearts, **every sin confessed in repentance** that needeth not to be repented of."
>
> *REFLECTING CHRIST,* PAGE 102

Question 4: What will be the result of taking these first three steps? Acts 1:8

Answer: ____

Just as the **Holy Spirit was poured** out on the praying, believing, confessing disciples, it will be poured out in our day. Once again the power of God will flow from His throne. God will raise up a last-day generation of witnesses. When the conditions are met, the promise will be fulfilled.

The more we know Christ, the more we long to share His love with others. The more we share His love, the more we long to know Him better. The more we love Him, the more we will witness. The more we witness, the more we love Him. **Witnessing to others is linked to our own spiritual growth.**

> "God could have reached His object in saving sinners without our aid; but in order for us to develop a character like Christ's, we must share in His work. In order to enter into His joy, the joy of seeing souls redeemed by His sacrifice, we must participate in His labors for their redemption."
>
> *THE DESIRE OF AGES,* PAGE 142

The outpouring of the Holy Spirit is promised to those who are seeking God for power to witness.

"The **Holy Spirit will come only** to all who are begging for the bread of life to give to their neighbors."

TESTIMONIES, VOLUME 6, PAGE 90

The Holy Spirit, Intercessory Prayer & Witnessing

Question 5: What are two essential ingredients in soul-winning? I John 5:14-16

Answer: 1. ______________________________

2. ______________________________

When we seek God in earnest intercession for others, He promises to make us a channel of His life-giving power. The river of water of life from God's throne is poured out through us to touch other hearts. Our prayers and our faith make a dramatic difference in their lives. Ellen White makes this very clear when she talks about these two essential ingredients.

"**Prayer and faith** will do what no power on earth can accomplish."

MINISTRY OF HEALING, PAGE 509

"It is a part of God's plan to grant us, in answer to the **prayer of faith**, that which He would not bestow did we not thus ask."

THE GREAT CONTROVERSY, PAGE 525

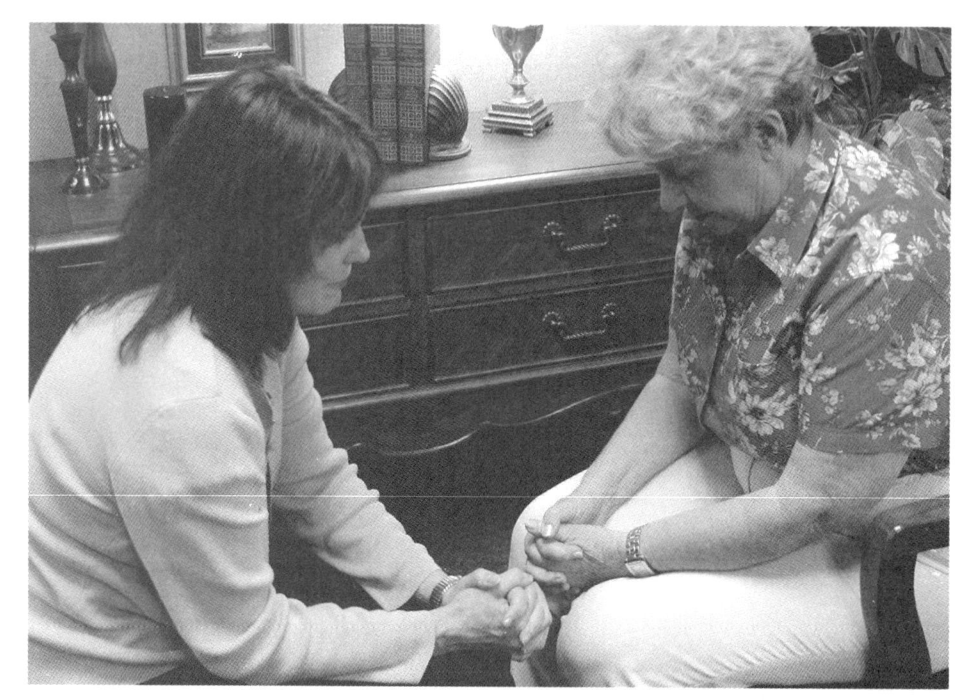

There are over 130 studies on the effectiveness of intercessory prayer and healing in the medical literature. Prayed-for people simply get well quicker, have fewer complications, need less medication and return to the hospital less. In the physical realm there is a dramatic difference when people are prayed for. If this is true in the physical realm, then it is certainly true in the spiritual realm as well.

Winning a soul is not like repairing an automobile or making a cake, for which there is a certain formula, and anyone who follows it will be successful. No, each person is different, and although there are **basic soul-winning principles** that apply to every situation, we **need the wisdom of God** in applying them. Otherwise, minds will not be impressed. Lives will be left unchanged.

Nothing can substitute for **prayers for souls**. No person can be won to Christ without prayer. Conversion is a miracle. Soul-winners are not simply convincing sales people pushing a product. We are dealing with the most precious thing in the world—people.

Four Reasons to Pray for Souls

Why is it necessary to pray for souls? Doesn't God already want to win them? Isn't He doing everything He can without our praying?

There is a great deal about the science of prayer that the human mind cannot comprehend. This should not discourage us. Not knowing everything about electricity does not keep us from employing the benefits of light, heat and electrical power.

Although we will never fully understand the science of prayer, **there are at least four reasons we should pray for souls.**

REASON 1

Prayer enables God to speak to us about the sins in our own lives that are a hindrance to successful soul-winning.

Question 6: What did David pray for in Psalm 51:10-12?

Answer:____

David longed for **purity of heart**. He hungered for the presence of God in His life. He yearned for the fullness of God's Spirit.

Question 7: What does David declare will be the result of a renewed experience with Jesus? Psalm 51:13

Answer: ____________________________________

A renewed experience with God leads to the **desire to share that experience with others**. An in-filling of His Spirit leads to an out-flowing of His love. Before God can do something with us, He must do something for us. Before God can do something through us, He must do something in us. God's power is limited when there is cherished sin in our own hearts. Often, as you and I pray for others, Jesus impresses our own hearts with the need of a closer fellowship with Him.

REASON 2

Prayer deepens our desire concerning the thing for which we are praying.

Question 8: What did Jesus pray for in Gethsemane? Matthew 26:39

Answer:____

One of the model intercessory prayers in the Bible is the one Jesus prayed for our salvation in Gethsemane. As the Savior prayed, He experienced a conflict with the powers of hell. On His knees He cried out, "If it is possible, let this cup pass from Me; nevertheless not as I will, but as You will."

There in the garden Jesus won the battle. His desire to save us intensified as He prayed. The thing that He prayed for—our salvation—became the all-consuming passion of His life. Surely He desired to save us before He prayed, but after His prayer His desire to save us was even stronger.

The more we pray for someone's salvation, the more we desire it. The more we desire it, the more we will look for creative opportunities to reach that person.

REASON 3

Prayer puts us in touch with divine wisdom.

Question 9: What does James promise to those who need wisdom? James 1:5

Answer: ____

The only One who is wise enough to win souls is God. Jesus reveals the right words to say to men and women. Without His wisdom we may have keys, but we do not know which key fits where. Only as Christ imparts wisdom to us will we know the right key to open hearts to receive the treasures of the gospel.

REASON 4

Prayer enables God to work more powerfully than He could if we did not pray.

Question 10: What does God promise those who seek Him in intercession?
Daniel 10:12 and James 5:16 (last part)

Answer: ____

As the Apostle James declares, "the effective fervent prayer" of a righteous person makes a dramatic difference. As the angel announced to Daniel, **"your words are heard."** When we intercede for others, life flows from the throne of God through us to touch other lives. In the great controversy between good and evil, we become God's channel of blessing.

Daniel 10 tells the story of how Daniel's prayers ascended to heaven for three weeks with no apparent answer. Yet at the end of those three weeks Gabriel explained to Daniel that a great battle had been going on over the mind of Cyrus. The good angels attempted to drive the evil angels back so that Cyrus could make the right decision. The evil angels attempted to destroy the good angels, to enshroud Cyrus in darkness. As Daniel prayed, this battle raged. Finally Jesus came down, beat the evil angels back, and gave Cyrus an opportunity to make a clear and intelligent decision—a decision that allowed Israel to go free. Daniel's intercessory prayer proved effective.

Question 11: What model of intercession does the apostle Paul give us?
Colossians 1:3 and Philippians 1:3-4

Answer: ____

The Apostle Paul remembered the churches he raised up through his evangelistic journeys. Daily he prayed for the churches at Galatia, Ephesus, Philippi, Colosse and Thessalonica.

Paul had his prayer list. He prayed for individuals by name. He prayed for churches and he prayed for individual cities. Do you have your prayer list? Are you praying for your loved ones by name? Are you holding up your community before God? **Soul-winning necessitates God's power to do God's work.**

Question 12: In addition to praying alone, what instruction did Jesus give us
about praying with others? Matthew 18:19-20

Answer: ____

Prayer bands provide the basis for successful evangelism. The work of conversion is not natural; it is supernatural. A salesman might be able to persuade a person to buy a new car. Advertising companies may entice an individual to purchase a new suit. A real estate broker might interest a person in an attractive new home. These sales people can get results by following certain techniques. They can sell their product. It might even be possible for a Christian minister to persuade a person to join the church.

But only God can bring genuine conversion to the soul. **Successful evangelism must include a ministry of prayer.**

> "Why do not two or three meet together and plead with God for the salvation of some special one, and then still another?"
>
> *TESTIMONIES,* VOLUME 7, PAGE 21

Take a moment right now and **write the names of people on the lines below that you think might be open to the gospel.** These people may be family members, work associates, friends, neighbors or casual acquaintances.

1. ______________________________

2. ______________________________

3. ______________________________

4. ______________________________

Seek God for these people each day. Write down their names and petition heaven for their souls. If possible, choose a prayer partner. Together bombard heaven with your prayers. God will answer. You will become a channel of His abundant blessing.

Prayer enables us to be sensitive to the Holy Spirit's leading. Prayer allows us to see with God's eyes. If we are going to reach people for Christ, we must understand how best to approach them, how to answer their questions and how best to appeal to them. Only God can lead us to the people we will be most effective in reaching.

To be the most affective witnesses for God, we are looking for people God has especially prepared for us to work with. Here are a few things to keep in mind.

- Every person in the world is not your assignment!
- Pray that God will **lead you** to the person He wants you to witness to.
- **Look** first at the people God brings into your life each day.
- Watch for opportunities to **share God's love** and observe their response.

> "**Begin to pray for souls**; come near to Christ, close to His bleeding side. Let a meek and quiet spirit adorn your lives, and let your earnest, broken, humble petitions ascend to Him for wisdom **that you may have success in saving not only your own soul, but the souls of others**."
>
> *TESTIMONIES,* VOLUME 1, PAGE 513

By asking we receive. The reason we often don't receive from God is because we don't ask. **We will have success in soul-winning when we begin to pray for souls**. You will become part of the fulfillment of this marvelous statement.

> "**Hundreds and thousands were seen visiting families and opening before them the word of God**. Hearts were convicted by the power of the Holy Spirit, and a spirit of genuine conversion was manifest."
>
> *TESTIMONIES,* VOLUME 9, PAGE 126

Since we are living in the days of earth's final harvest, it is essential to consecrate ourselves to God for service. **The success of any Bible study work or evangelistic campaign is dependent on the Holy Spirit**.

As pastors and lay people unite together in an integrated, coordinated approach in winning souls for Christ, praying for the mighty outpouring of the Holy Spirit, God will give unusual results. **The Holy Spirit will be poured out and souls will be won**.

PRACTICAL WAYS TO BEGIN A PRAYER MINISTRY IN YOUR CHURCH

- Select a prayer ministry leader and co-leader.
- The leader and co-leader each prayerfully select two people to join them.
- Select people who have a burden for intercession.
- Select people who will commit to meet once a week to pray.
- Ask those four people to each invite another person to join them in the same commitment. (There are now ten people composing one prayer group.)
- Pray for specific names.
- Use the *Intercessory Prayer Guide*.
- List three to five names of people you wish to pray for inside the *Intercessory Prayer Guide*.
- Pray for them daily.
- Join the *Soup & Salvation* program.
- Meet once a week for twelve weeks.
- Study *Prayer Warriors* or other material on the power of prayer.
- Pray! Pray! Pray! (You can use the principles of "Conversational Prayer" found in Appendix C.)

On the next page is a sample of the ***Intercessory Prayer Guide***.

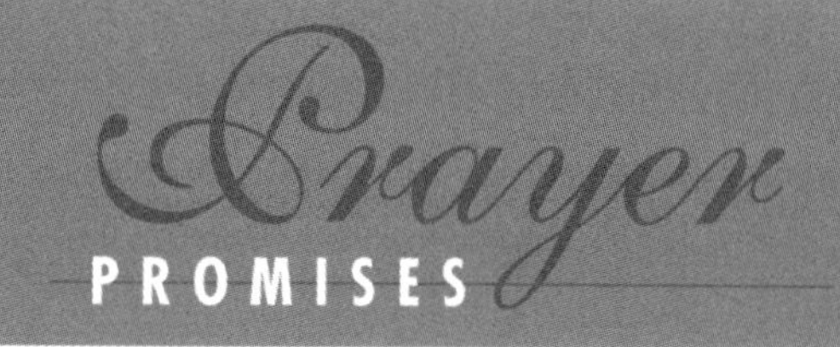

"The effectual fervent prayer of a righteous man availeth much." James 5:16

"...If any man see his brother sin a sin which is not unto death, he shall ask and He shall give him life for them that sin not unto death." 1 John 5:16

"Ask and it shall be given you." Matthew 7:7

"Prayer and faith will do what no power on earth can accomplish." Ministry of Healing, p. 509

"God will do in answer to the prayer of faith that which He would not do did we not thus ask." Great Controversy, p. 525

For additional prayer guides please contact:

It Is Written
P.O. Box 0
Thousand Oak, CA 91360
or visit: www.iiw.org

Why Intercessory Prayer?

In the great controversy between good and evil, God has established some basic ground rules. He will not violate freedom of choice. He does everything he can to save each individual. He sends His angels. The Holy Spirit impresses hearts. He arranges circumstances in each life. But He only goes so far. Intercessory Prayer unleashes heaven's power. God honors our choice for others. His life-giving love is poured out through us to them.

Intercessory Prayer is also a channel for God's wisdom to flow through us to reach others. He provides us with the knowledge to share His love. He gives us the keys to their hearts.

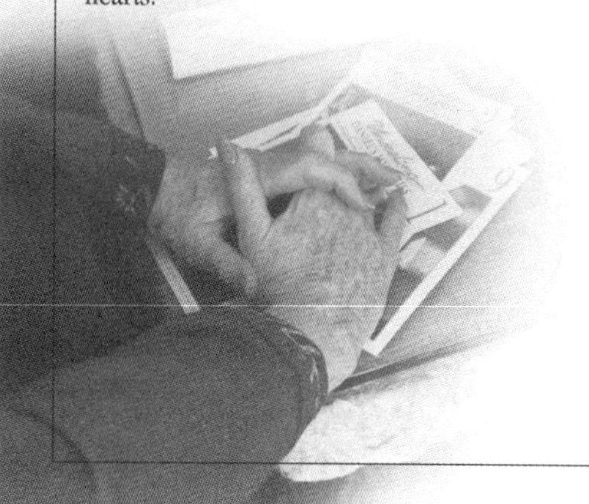

How to Use This Prayer Guide

■ 1. Choose 3-5 people whom you will pray for daily in the next month.

■ 2. Ask the Lord for wisdom to do something kind for them within the next two weeks.

> *"If we would humble ourselves before God and be kind and courteous and tenderhearted and pitiful, there would be 100 conversions where there is now one."* Testimonies, Vol. 9, p. 189

■ 3. Seek God for wisdom to know how best to reach them for him.

■ 4. Two weeks before the evangelistic crusade, deliver the handbill and invite them to the meeting. Be sure to sign them up for a reserved seat.

■ 5. Attend the evangelistic meetings regularly with them.

My Prayer List

____

____

____

____

____

CHAPTER 4

THE POWER OF GOD'S WORD

Many years ago the renowned English preacher, George Whitfield, was an overnight houseguest of a wealthy, aristocratic family. They had everything except the One who counts for everything. They were kind, hospitable people, but they did not know Christ. Whitfield longed to share the Christ he loved with them.

When he awoke the next morning, sun streamed through his bedroom window. Whitfield noted an exquisite diamond ring on the nightstand by his bed. He took the ring and etched in the windowpane those familiar words from the story of the rich young ruler, "One thing thou lackest." He said nothing to the lady of the house. After breakfast he graciously thanked his host and hostess and left.

When the nobleman and his wife discovered what Whitfield had done, they were irate. Soon their anger turned to curiosity. They searched through Scripture. They discovered the story of the rich young ruler. Their hearts were touched. Those four words of Scripture burned their way into their souls.

"One thing thou lackest." Together they knelt and surrendered their lives to Christ. The Bible is powerful. It changes lives. It transforms people. The Bible is God's dynamic agency for soul-winning.

The same Holy Spirit that prompted the writers of Scripture to pen **God's word transforms the lives of those who read God's word.**

At creation, God's audible word carried with it the power to create matter.

"By the word of the Lord were the heavens made; and all the host of them by the breath of His mouth."
Psalm 33:6

What God says is so, even if it were never so before, because **God has the power to accomplish what He declares**. Ellen White in the book *Education* affirms the power of the word of God to change lives.

> "**The creative energy that called the worlds into existence is in the word of God**. This word imparts power; it begets life. Every command is a promise; accepted by the will, received into the soul, it brings with it the life of the Infinite One. **It transforms the nature** and recreates the soul in the image of God."
>
> *EDUCATION*, PAGE 126

What a truth! **The creative power of God is in His word. When we share God's word with others, God's creative power flows into their lives**. Mark Finley, in his book *Persuasion*, says:

> "The **life-giving promises and principles of the word of God carry with them the power to do that which they declare**. Since God's word is living, it not only presents the way to live, but it carries with it the power to accomplish right living."
>
> *PERSUASION*, PAGE 13

There is no other book that carries as much power as the word of God. When you and I open our Bibles and read a text containing the words of God with them, we have a powerful agency that will bring about change in their lives.

Question 1: Where do successful soul-winners find their strength?
Matthew 4:4 and Jeremiah 15:16

Answer ____

Jesus met Satan's temptations with the word of God. Jeremiah declared God's word nourished his soul. When we feed on God's word, God Himself nourishes our spiritual life. God's word will give us courage, faith and a new energy.

What if the tree of life from the Garden of Eden was present in a remote, hidden valley a few hundred miles from your home? Would you make an effort to find it to eat and be renewed? What if the branches of the tree of life hung over heaven's walkway right into your backyard? Would you be interested in plucking some of heaven's life-giving fruit?

Here is an almost unbelievable truth:

"So with all the **promises of God's word**. In them He is speaking to us individually, speaking as directly as if we could listen to His voice. It is in these promises that Christ communicates to us His grace and power. They are leaves from that tree which is 'for the healing of the nations.' (Revelation 22:2) Received, assimilated, they are to be the strength of the character, the inspiration and sustenance of the life. **Nothing else can have such healing power. Nothing besides can impart the courage and faith which give vital energy to the whole being.**"

MINISTRY OF HEALING, PAGE 122

Question 2: Where does the power to transform lives come from?
James 1:21-22; 2 Peter 1:2-4

Answer____

Whenever you and I go into the homes of our friends and neighbors and open God's word, we are sharing principles that transform lives.

The word of God is so powerful that it can change people even if we are novices in giving Bible studies, and we make mistakes or stumble in the process.

Ernestine Finley tells a fascinating story about her evangelist husband, Mark:

Mark was a senior theology student at Atlantic Union College. One of his theology class requirements instructed him to find someone to go through a complete series of Bible studies with him. In order to graduate with a degree in theology, he had to complete the assignment. He looked around and finally managed to find a dear, sweet lady, named Mae, who would tolerate his studying with her.

Mark was nervous and very unsure of himself. But week after week he went to her home sharing the word of God. He sometimes stumbled through the lesson, but managed to finish the entire 29-lesson series. He felt that this first series of Bible studies was a failure. The lady he studied with asked questions, but made no visible decisions. Her life generally seemed the same.

Although Mark finished an entire series of Bible studies and did complete his theology degree requirements, he was a little disappointed with the results of the Bible study.

After graduation, he began his ministry in the Southern New England Conference. Ten years later, he returned to Atlantic Union College as the conference evangelist to hold a series of evangelistic meetings. The meetings were conducted in the newly-built Field House at the college.

Advertising brochures were mailed to the communities around the college. People came. In fact, over 1,000 people attended on opening night. After his sermon, he saw a familiar lady walking down the aisle. It was the same dear lady he studied the Bible with as a student ten years before. She complemented him on his sermon and said, "My, you sure have changed in ten years!"

Yes, he had changed from an unsure, timid student to a dynamic preacher for Christ! That night, Mark and I prayed for her earnestly. He told the Lord that this lady had been waiting for ten years, but the seed of the word of God had been planted. He asked that the seeds of truth sown so feebly ten years ago might now bear fruit.

They did, and Mae was one of the first ones baptized in that Atlantic Union College evangelistic series. The time was right. Mae's heart was open, and she eagerly grasped Bible truth.

THERE IS POWER IN THE WORD OF GOD.

God uses us even when we feel inadequate. The **power** is not in us. It is **in God's word**. If we will begin sharing our faith with others, although we have limitations, God will still work in a powerful way through us. Hearts will be touched. Lives will be changed. **The power of God's word is life-transforming**.

Question 3: Why is God's word so powerful in changing lives? Hebrews 4:12

Answer:____

God's word is alive and powerful. The same Holy Spirit that inspired the Bible transforms our lives when we read it.

God's promises are true. He will fulfill His word. Whenever we share God's word, we impart principles that transform and heal lives.

Pastor Mark Finley shares this experience in his book, *Persuasion*, Pages 13-14:

A former Seventh-day Adventist attended one of his evangelistic meetings in New England. As he visited in her home one evening, he talked to her about returning to the family of God. Her eyes glistened as she replied, "I'd like to, but I can't. I smoke."

He called her by name and asked, "Do you believe that Jesus wants you to have victory over this habit?"

"Oh, yes, I do. But I can't. I'm just too weak."

He said, "May I read you a Bible text?" He opened his Bible to I John 5:14, "This is the confidence that we have in Him, that if we ask anything according to his will, He hears us."

"Now, Mary, do you have confidence that you can quit smoking?" he asked.

"No." she replied.

"Good," he said, "because the Bible says, 'This is the confidence we have in Him.' So where is the confidence?"

She replied, "In Him."

He read the text once more adding, "If we ask anything according to His will, *except give up smoking, he hears us*."

Turning to Mary he asked, "Should I write that in your Bible? Can I have your Bible to write it there?"

"No, no," she said, "I don't want to change the Bible."

He said, "Is it according to God's will for you to quit smoking?"

"Yes, it is," she replied.

"Then, can you ask Christ in confidence for the power He has promised?"

"Oh, yes, she responded, "I believe I can."

"I have one more question: When will you receive this power to give up smoking? Will it be in a week, a month, three months? When will you receive that power?"

He then opened his Bible and turned to John 1:12 and read, " 'As many as received Him, to them gave he power to become the sons of God.' To receive Jesus is to receive the power. Now, tonight we have seen that you can have confidence in Jesus. We have seen that whatever we ask according to His will, He will give us. And we know it is His will for you to give up smoking. We have seen as well, that as you receive Him, you will receive power."

Mary sat quietly. A new light came into her eyes. Pastor Finley then said, "Tonight, would you like to kneel here and tell Jesus that you have confidence in Him to do for you what you can't do for yourself? Would you like to tell Him that you believe it is His will for you to quit smoking? Would you like to receive power right now, believing by faith that He is giving it to you? That, in spite of any craving, through the power of Christ you will have the victory, because His word says it? By faith, would you like to believe what God says?"

They knelt and Mary prayed. That night God gave Mary total victory over smoking three packs of cigarettes a day.

Certainly Pastor Finley suggested some very practical principles to help her quit smoking, but through claiming the promises in the word of God she found true deliverance in Christ.

She needed someone to help her believe God's word and claim His promises by faith so she could gain the victory over smoking.

THE SCRIPTURES CHANGE LIVES BECAUSE

THE WORD OF GOD IS ETERNALLY ENDURING

It lasts from generation to generation.

Isaiah 40:8 – "The grass withers, the flower fades, but the word of our God stands forever."

Mathew 24:35 – "Heaven and earth will pass away, but My words will never pass away."

THE WORD OF GOD IS UNIVERSALLY APPLICABLE

The word of God applies to every kindred, nation, tongue and people.

Matthew 24:14 – "And this gospel of the kingdom will be preached in all the world as a witness to all the nations then the end shall come."

Revelation 14:6 – "Then I saw another angel flying in the midst of heaven, having the everlasting gospel to preach to those who dwell on the earth—to every nation, tribe, tongue, and people."

THE WORD OF GOD IS LIFE-TRANSFORMING

God's word has the power to convert hearts and minds.

I Peter 1:23 – "Having been born again, not of corruptible seed but incorruptible, through the word of God which lives and abides forever."

Psalm 119:11 – "Your word I have hidden in my heart, that I might not sin against you."

THE WORD OF GOD IS DIVINELY-INSPIRED

Many books may be inspiring, but God's word is inspired.

2 Timothy 3:16 – "All Scripture is given by inspiration of God, and is profitable for doctrine, for reproof, for correction, for instruction in righteousness."

John 17:17 – "Sanctify them by your truth. Your word is truth."

THE WORD OF GOD IS LIFE-GIVING

The word of God contains the divine life-giving power of the Holy Spirit.

Psalm 119:50 – "For your word has given me life."

Deuteronomy 8:3 – "But man lives by every word that proceeds from the mouth of the Lord."

THE WORD OF GOD MELTS HARD HEARTS

The word of God burns away the dross in our lives through the purifying presence of the Holy Spirit.

Jeremiah 23:29 – "'Is not My word like a fire?' says the Lord, 'and like a hammer that breaks the rock in pieces?'"

God's word burns like a fire. It consumes sin. It melts hard hearts. Commit yourself to sharing the life-transforming principles of God's word with others. Their hearts will be touched. You will be amazed at how God's word penetrates darkened minds. You will be amazed at how God's word breaks hard hearts. You will be amazed at how God's word inspires men and women to lift their vision from earth below to heaven above.

God's promises in His word are sure. He will do what His word declares. **We need a revival in Bible study**. A knowledge of God will cover the entire earth and when this happens, hearts and lives will be changed throughout the world.

> "A **revival in Bible study is needed** throughout the world. Attention is to be called, not to the assertions of men, but to the word of God. As this is done, a mighty work will be wrought. When God declared that His word should not return unto Him void, He meant all that He said. The gospel is to be preached to all nations. The Bible is to be opened to the people. A knowledge of God is the highest education, and it will cover the earth with its wonderful truth as the waters cover the sea."
>
> *MANUSCRIPT 139,* 1898

This program will help you experience first-hand the power in the word.

The word has life-giving, life-changing power. Work to plant it in people's minds and there will be an abundant harvest of souls through your ministry. As you share, you too will grow.

GOD'S WORD IS POWERFUL!

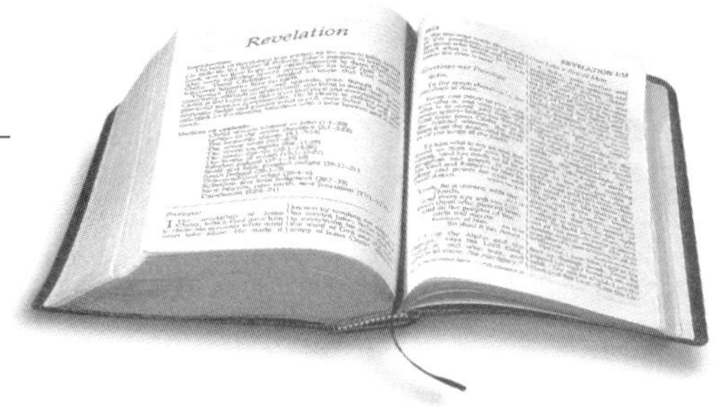

FASCINATING FACTS ABOUT THE BIBLE

- As many as 40 authors wrote the Bible over a period of more than 1,500 years (from 1500 B.C. to about A.D. 100.)
- The 40 authors differed widely in their cultures and education, and in their personalities and intellectual perceptions—yet the books they wrote do not contradict one another!
- There are 39 books in the Old Testament. If you multiply those two digits together (3x9) you will have the number of books in the New Testament, 27.
- The Bible was divided into chapters in the middle of the thirteenth century.
- The verse divisions were introduced in 1551.

CHAPTER 5

KEYS FOR FINDING AND DEVELOPING INTERESTS

In every community, God is at work opening hearts to the gospel. Before we ever begin looking for interested people, God is stirring their hearts to create an interest in divine things. The art of finding Bible study interests is the art of discovering people in whose heart God has already created an interest. There are some very practical ways in which we can cooperate with God to find people who are interested in studying His word.

Many people are hungering to know truth. They are waiting for someone to explain the Bible to them. Ellen White shares this encouraging thought:

> "All over the world men and women are looking wistfully to heaven. Prayers and tears and inquiries go up from souls longing for light, for grace, for the Holy Spirit. Many are on the verge of the kingdom, waiting only to be gathered in."
>
> *ACTS OF THE APOSTLES*, PAGE 109

It is heaven's desire to link up these praying seekers longing for light and truth with witnessing Christians.

In this chapter we will learn a variety of ways to discover new interests. These methods will help you find a steady stream of people interested in learning more about the Bible.

BIBLICAL PRINCIPLES FOR FINDING INTERESTS

The Psalmist David gives us three vital principles for finding interests:

> "Those who sow in tears shall reap in joy. He who continually **goes forth weeping, bearing seed for sowing**, shall doubtless come again with rejoicing, bringing his sheaves with him."
>
> *PSALM 126:5-6*

Question 1: What is the first vital principle the Psalmist gives us in discovering interests? Psalm 126:6 (first part)

Answer____

The first principle in finding interested people for God's kingdom **is "going forth."** In ancient times people lived in walled cities for protection. Their fields were outside the cities. Each morning when the gates of the cities were opened, farmers went out to work in the fields. To be successful in soul-winning it is necessary to "go forth." This "going forth" has two dimensions.

There is the **psychological "going forth."** Someone once said, "Anyone wrapped up in himself is a very small package." The reason there are so few real soul-winners is because so few people are willing to look out of themselves to minister to the needs of others. Ask God to help you "go out" of yourself. Ask Him to open your eyes for the special person He wants you to share His love with.

The second aspect of "going forth" is a **physical "going forth**." Souls are not won unless we "go out" to where people are. Jesus mingled with people. The disciples mingled with people. Soul-winners "go out." They mingle with people **knocking on doors, visiting homes, seeking opportunities everywhere to witness**.

> "There are families who will never be reached by the truths of God's word unless the stewards of His grace enter their homes and point them to the higher way."
>
> *ACTS OF THE APOSTLES*, PAGE 363

PRACTICAL STEPS TO APPLY THE "GOING-FORTH" PRINCIPLE

Here are some practical steps you can take to apply this "going-forth" principle:

- Set aside some time each week to witness for your Lord.
- Although witnessing is part of your daily lifestyle, set aside time to seek out people that you may not come in contact with in the normal flow of your daily activities.
  — Through visitation ministry.
  — Through literature ministry.
- Develop new ways to discover interests. (See Page 48 for several ways to discover interests.)

In most instances, people will not come knocking on our doors seeking for truth; we must knock on their doors. They will not walk into our churches; we must walk into their homes. They will not seek us; we must seek them. They will not come to us; we must go to them.

Church is the place where our souls are spiritually nourished and where we are equipped to serve. The world is the place where our witness makes the gospel authentic. We come to church to receive spiritual strength and training in witnessing so we can go into the world like Jesus did to win people for the kingdom.

Question 2: In the second principle, what emotion does David describe as essential to soul-winning? Psalm 126:6

Answer:____

Just as seed needs water to germinate and grow, **soul-winning requires the water of our tears**. What is this weeping? It is certainly not some emotionally-charged crying. This "weeping" Scripture speaks about is a heartfelt burden to win lost people which leads to earnest intercession. It is a genuine concern for the lost. It is a divinely sanctified passion for the unsaved.

When William Booth, the founder of the Salvation Army, was invited to visit the queen in Buckingham Palace in London, England he wrote these words in the guest book:

> "Your majesty, some men's ambition is fame,
> Some men's ambition is power,
> Some men's ambition is money,
> My ambition is the souls of men."

This is the passion that motivates all true soul-winners.

Question 3: What is the third key principle for finding interests? Psalm 126:6 (last part)

Answer:____

Every farmer knows the importance of sowing. What farmer could possibly expect to reap a harvest if he does not sow any seeds? The more we sow the more we will reap. This same principle applies in God's spiritual garden. God cannot bless any literature we do not distribute. He cannot bless brochures we have not mailed, Bible studies we have not given or evangelistic seminars we have not conducted. **Some churches expect to win souls without spending time sowing the seed**. They are only fooling themselves. In God's garden, the only seeds that grow are the ones we have sown. **God invites us to sow the seed** by passing out literature, visiting homes, knocking on doors, conducting small groups, distributing audio and videotapes, lending books, enrolling people in the Bible course and a host of other ways of sharing our faith.

Question 4: In the parable of the sower, what does Jesus say the seed represents? Luke 8:11

Answer: ____

The seed is God's word. When we go out of ourselves and go out into the community with our hearts filled with a love for people, sharing God's word, God promises to give us results.

Question 5: What promise does God make for those who follow these soul-winning principles? Psalm 126:6

Answer: ____

The word "doubtless" is a wonderful word. It means "without a doubt." Here is something you can be confident of; follow these simple steps and God will give you results.

When we "go forth" we will have results. The Bible teaches this in Psalm 126:5-6. As we sow in tears and continually go forth weeping, we shall doubtless come with rejoicing bringing our sheaves with us.

PRACTICAL STEPS TO DEVELOP THE ATTITUDE OF A SOUL-WINNER

Here are some practical steps you can take to develop the attitude of a soul-winner.

1. Ask God to give you the desire to witness

❦ Spend some time alone asking God to give you a greater desire to witness for Him.

2. Ask God for opportunities to witness to specific people

❦ Specifically ask Him to place a desire in your heart to witness to a few special people.

3. Lift these individuals up in prayer

❦ Lift the individuals up by name before God in prayer; seeking God's wisdom to approach them.

PRACTICAL WAYS TO DISCOVER AND DEVELOP INTERESTS

There are several ways of discovering interests. Each of the methods below will help you discover potential prospects for Bible studies. By using multiple methods, you will increase your chances of discovering many more prospects. The more opportunities you provide for the Holy Spirit to bring people into contact with truth, the more interested people He can lead to your church.

1. Develop an interest file

It is important to develop and update an interest file. Interests come from a variety of sources. First, make a list of all the family, friends and co-workers of Seventh-day Adventist church members. Interests may also come from previous evangelistic meetings or seminars at your church. Those who visit your church who are not members should also be placed in the interest file. (The topic of the interest file is so important that we have placed an entire section on how to develop and cultivate your interest file in the appendix. See Page124.)

The goal is to visit as many people as possible from the interest file, developing relationships leading to Bible study interests.

2. Follow up all media interests in your community

The media ministries of the Seventh-day Adventist Church will supply names of interests in your area. You can fill out the form in the appendix on Page 143 requesting those names. You can then visit these people by delivering one of Mark Finley's books and an enrollment card for the free Bible course. There is also an *It Is Written* survey in the appendix on Page 136 that you can use as you visit interests.

3. Make systematic mass mailings

The use of systematic mass mailings will produce new and fresh interests. This will provide an excellent base for new interests. There are a variety of Bible study enrollment cards you can use. Here are four examples:

- *Search for Certainty* Jesus Cards
- *Discover* Cards
- *Understanding Bible Prophecy* Cards
- *Something Wonderful* Cards

You will find an entire section on how to follow up Bible enrollment cards and deliver the Bible lessons in the Appendix beginning on Page 144.

4. Conduct door-to-door surveys

This is an excellent method of finding people with whom to study the Bible. The following surveys are in the appendix on Pages 136-138:

- *It Is Written* visitation survey approach
- *It Is Written* visitation book approach
- Community religious survey

5. Conduct felt-need programs

Felt-need programs are an excellent way of getting new interests. It is important to connect these programs with a reaping series of meetings or offer the participants the opportunity of taking Bible studies. The following are a few ideas of the felt-need programs you can conduct before an evangelistic series of meetings.

- Stress Management (*Managing Life's Stress*)
- Cooking School (*Natural Lifestyle Cooking*)
- Health Expo (*Newstart*)

Note: Materials for these seminars can be ordered through *It Is Written Television*.

Bridge-building – From felt-need programs to the spiritual dimension.

- **Develop new friendships**

During the felt-need programs you will develop many new friendships. Personal relationships are the pathway to introducing your friends to Jesus. As your participants develop confidence in what you have to share regarding health, they will develop confidence in what you share about the spiritual dimensions.

- **Be observant to spiritual openings**

During the felt-need programs, a group of church members should be observant and sensitive to spiritual openings.

- **Present cyclical programming**

Cyclical programs are a series of health programs conducted in a planned pattern. In this system, the participants of one program are invited to attend the next series of meetings, and are immediately enrolled if interested.

- **Provide opportunities**

Give the program participants an opportunity to register for other programs, seminars or Bible studies. During the felt-need seminar pass out the follow-up form entitled, "Yours for the Asking." (A copy of this is in the appendix on Page 140.)

6. Conduct home Bible study seminars

Conducting a home Bible seminar will often stimulate an interest in further Bible study. This will open the way for you to invite participants to have regular studies. The following seminars can be successfully conducted:

— *Unsealing Daniel's Mysteries*
— *Discover Jesus*

Beginning a home Bible seminar group

• Select a leader – Select a home Bible seminar leader and a co-leader.
• Invite church members – Invite four additional church members to join the group.
• Invite non-Adventist guests – Each of the six church members invites one non-Adventist guest to join. (This composes a group of 12 people.)
• Develop a schedule – The once-a-week schedule below is a format we have found successful.

7:30-7:45 p.m.	Getting-acquainted time
7:45-7:50 p.m.	Prayer time before studying God's word
7:50-8:35 p.m.	Show videotape (*Unsealing Daniel's Mysteries*)
8:35-8:50 p.m.	Lesson review/questions
8:50-9:00 p.m.	Close/goodbye

• Acquire Pre-enrollments – Give each participant the opportunity to register for the evangelistic series. On week 10, pass out brochures and reservation tickets for the evangelistic meetings. (See the Pre-Registration form for reserved seats in the appendix Page 153.)

You can make a difference in the lives of scores of people as you invite them to your home to study the word of God in a home group setting.

7. Begin a literature ministry

Placing literature in the hands of people will stimulate an interest in further Bible study. Literature ministry is a proven method of developing Bible study interests.

> "The **press is a powerful means to move the minds and hearts of the people**...if men, under the influence of the spirit of the world and of Satan, are earnest to circulate books, tracts, and papers of a corrupting nature, you should be more earnest to get reading matter of an elevating and saving character before the people. God has placed at the command of His people advantages in the press, which, combined with other agencies, will be successful in extend-

ing the knowledge of the truth. **Tracts, papers, and books, as the case demands, should be circulated in all the cities and villages in the land.**"

LIFE SKETCHES, PAGES 216-217

See *Soup & Salvation*, Page 80, for details on beginning a literature ministry in your church.

8. Begin a tape lending ministry

A tape-lending ministry distributes Biblical lectures on audiocassettes, videotapes and digital video discs (DVD). This ministry is an exciting way to cultivate interests, because it's an easy method lay members can use to share their faith with others.

How to begin

Advertise – The tape library should be advertised well. Distribute a flyer or door knocker which includes all essential information about available tapes.

Follow up – Follow up by returning to the area. Knock on the door and ask if they received the flyer. (This is a opportunity to find out who is interested.)

Leave audio or videotapes – When a person is interested, leave the audio or videotape with them. Tell them it is on a loan basis and you will return for it.

Return in a week – Tell them you will be back in one week to pick up the tape and leave another one. This can lead to a new friendship and an active Bible study.

What to say

"Hello, my name is ________________. We represent *It Is Written Television*, and we stopped by to give you an opportunity to view this video.

"In the world we live in, people have many questions about life today, and which way this world is headed. Some wonder what happens when a person dies. Others wonder why there is so much pain and suffering in our world.

"Mark Finley, speaker for *It Is Written Television*, has produced videos and audiotapes that answer these questions.

"I'll be happy to leave this video with you. There is no cost or obligation. We will simply loan it to you and pick it up next week.

"It has been a pleasure talking with you today. Thank you so much. See you next week."

9. Spontaneously share Christ

God often prepares people for our witness ahead of time. Look for opportunities throughout your day to share Christ. As you come in contact with people at work, school or during your recreational activities, ask God to open your eyes to **see people as winnable**. As you spontaneously share Christ, doors will open for Bible studies. Witnessing will become a part of your life. God is already at work opening hearts to the gospel. As you use these keys for finding and developing interests, God will give you wonderful results.

CHAPTER 6

AN EFFECTIVE PLAN FOR GIVING BIBLE STUDIES

Early Christians were passionate about sharing Bible truths with others. The Apostle Peter visited Cornelius' own house and taught him the truth about Jesus. Philip met privately with the Ethiopian, explaining to him truths of prophecy. Paul sat down in the ruins of the Philippian jail after an earthquake and unfolded the truth about Jesus to the Philippian jailer and his entire family. Aquilla and Pricilla, Corinthian church members, seized the opportunity to explain the truth to others. Through their ministry, Appollos accepted the new light of truth regarding Jesus.

The book of Acts describes one of the most significant reasons there were tens of thousands converted in the first century. "And daily in the temple and in every house, they did not cease teaching and preaching Jesus as the Christ." (Acts 5:42) These early disciples preached in public buildings such as the synagogues. They also taught people privately in their homes." Each Christian shared the truths he/she had learned with their friends and neighbors. This house-to-house ministry of the word led to an explosion of church growth.

Each revival in the history of Christianity has been accompanied by a corresponding revival of lay witnessing. This was true in the Reformation, the Weslyian Revival and certainly the Advent Movement.

Adventist believers wanted to share their faith. The Lord led the Seventh-day Adventist Church into an emphasis on the question-and-answer method of Bible studies through an amazing chain of circumstances.

At a **campmeeting held in 1882** in the state of California, a severe storm arose while Elder S.N. Haskell was preaching. The heavy downfall of the rain and the roar of the thunder made so much noise that the people in the tent could not hear Elder Haskell. The service had to be discontinued. It was at that time, that Elder Haskell gathered a group of people around him in the center of the tent. Since it was impossible to preach, Elder Haskell **gave out texts of Scripture to different people to read**. He began asking questions concerning the truths stated in the texts read.

The Spirit of the Lord was present, and in a very remarkable manner Bible truths were impressed on the minds of the people. As a result of this experience, Elder Haskell concluded

that this plan of studying the Bible would be an excellent way to present the truth to families and small groups of people.

Ellen White was in attendance at this camp meeting, and although she was not present at Elder Haskell's meeting, she was told of the experience. She was greatly interested. The next day, in an interview with Elder Haskell, **Mrs. White stated that the plan of Bible study that had been followed was in harmony with the light she had received**. She was convinced God Himself led Elder Haskell to answer, directly from the Bible, the questions people were asking.

Question 1: What is an effective plan of giving Bible Studies? Isaiah 28:9-10

Answer: ____

____

God has placed all of the truths necessary for salvation in His word. The Bible is a library of truth. **Effective Bible studies link key texts together on a single subject** that reveal Bible truths about that specific topic.

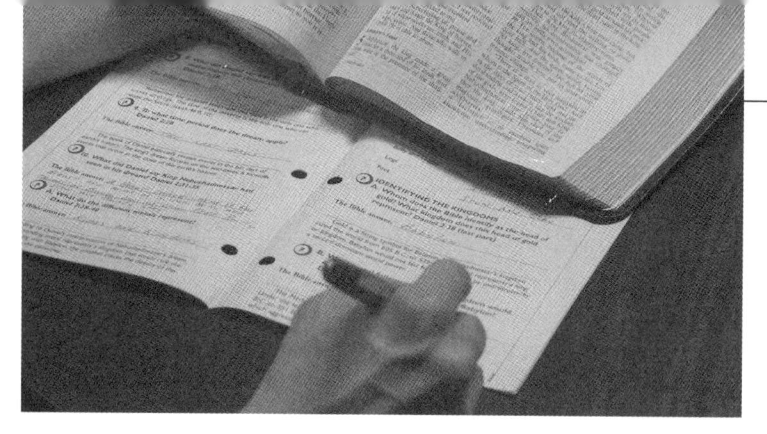

Using a set of lessons that have been constructed into textual outlines is very important. There is power in our instruction when this method is used. This helps our students realize that truth is more than just another idea of a Christian church—it comes directly out of Scripture.

> "**The best work you can do is to teach, to educate**. Whenever you can find an opportunity to do so, sit down with some family, and let them ask questions. Then answer them patiently, humbly...take your Bible, and open before them its great truths. Your success will not depend so much upon your knowledge and accomplishments, as upon your ability to find your way to the heart."
>
> *GOSPEL WORKERS*, PAGE 193

Question 2: Whose wisdom do we seek in giving Bible studies? How do we discover the Holy Spirit's wisdom? I Corinthians 2:13

Answer: A.______________________________

B. ______________________________

It is very important to **seek the Holy Spirit** when we are involved in Bible study ministry. The question-and-answer method of giving Bible studies, **comparing spiritual things with spiritual things**, is a heaven-born idea. Using this method, workers are developed who will become mighty men of God. This is confirmed in the book *Gospel Workers.*

> "The plan of holding Bible readings was a **heaven-born idea**. There are many, both men and women, who can engage in this branch of missionary labor. Workers may thus be developed who will become mighty men of God. By this means the word of God has been given to thousands; and the workers are brought into personal contact with people of all nations and tongues."
>
> *GOSPEL WORKERS*, PAGE 192

No book carries as much power as the word of God for enabling men and women to make decisions; no method is a powerful as taking the texts of the Bible and applying them in real-life situations. We can give our opinions, even say, "I think..." or, "My church teaches..." but it carries very little weight. However, **when we open our Bibles and read a text that tells people what God says, we have enlisted powerful agencies for change to take place in their lives.**

Question 3: When Jesus wanted to convince the two disciples on Emmaus Road that He was the Messiah, how did He do it? Luke 24:27, 44

Answer: ____

____

Jesus did not work a miracle to convince two of His disciples that He was the Messiah. **He gave them a Bible study**. Jesus began with the first five books of the Bible—the writings of Moses—and traced the prophecies in the Old Testament text-by-text that proved He was the Messiah.

One of the most effective methods of teaching Bible truth is the plan of B**ible studies in the home in question-and-answer form**. These weekly visits to the home establish the confidence of the family in the worker and in the Scriptures and pave the way for the presentation and acceptance of the testing truths.

The question-and-answer plan of giving Bible studies is a simple, easy, yet extremely powerful method.

GENERAL PRINCIPLES FOR GIVING BIBLE STUDIES

Principle 1: Use a good series of simple Bible studies

It is not necessary to write your own set of Bible studies. There are many good, solid, proven sets of studies that have been field-tested. We recommend Pastor Finley's *Search for Certainty* series.

The *Search for Certainty* series presents each Bible truth as a link in a connected chain. The lessons are systematically arranged—one lesson flows logically into the next.

> "God is leading out a people and establishing them upon the one great platform of faith, the commandments of God and the testimony of Jesus. He has given His people a straight chain of Bible truth, clear and connected. This truth is of heavenly origin and has been searched for as for hidden treasure. It has been dug out through careful searching of the Scriptures and through much prayer."
>
> *TESTIMONIES,* VOLUME 3, PAGE 447

Principle 2: Have a distinct plan

When giving Bible studies, determine to have a distinct plan before you teach any subject. It is important that you understand each subject yourself. Then you will be able to clearly present these Biblical truths to others.

> "Before attempting to teach a subject, he should have a distinct plan in mind, and should know just what he desires to accomplish. He should not rest satisfied with the presentation of any subject until the student understands the principle involved, perceives its truth, and is able to state clearly what he has learned."
>
> *EDUCATION*, PAGES 233-234

Practical advice

- Follow the same **basic sequence** with all interests.
- **Don't skip** a study even if the student says he/she already knows the subject.
- **Be sure** the person understands the subject clearly before going on to another subject.

The "clear and set principle" that Mark Finley talks about in his book *Persuasion* will help to illustrate the importance of the Bible student's knowledge of the subject.

The "clear and set principle" teaches that only as new truths are clarified and confirmed in the minds of the listeners can future truths be received and accepted.

The presenter must ascertain, at every new step, whether the hearer accepts or rejects the message, and how they have decided to integrate these new concepts into their present value structure.

If this is not done, resistance will continue to build to the point of rejection. Truth, and the acceptance of truth, is progressive.

> "Many a laborer fails in his work because he does not come close to those who most need his help. With the Bible in hand, he should seek in a courteous manner to **learn the objections which exist in the minds of those who are beginning to inquire, "What is truth?"** Carefully and tenderly should he lead and educate them, as pupils in a school."
>
> *GOSPEL WORKERS*, PAGE 190

Here is an example of how to apply the "clear and set principle" in a Bible study on salvation.

Question: *"Have you ever understood the plan of salvation before or is this new to you?"*
Answer: "Yes, I've heard about Christ, but I've never studied the plan of salvation from the Bible."
Question: *"Do you have any questions about salvation? Is it clear to you?"*
Answer: "Yes, it is so much clearer after the study today. Before I studied it from the Bible, I always thought I had to earn my salvation; or, I thought that if I were only good enough, then I could be saved."
Question: *"Now do you understand that salvation is a gift, which you can accept right now by faith?"*
Answer: "Yes"
Question: *"Would you like to accept Jesus right now and ask Him to come into your life?"*

Get the points and texts fastened in the minds of your Bible students. Let them ask questions, and then answer them in the plainest, simplest manner possible so they can grasp the truths presented.

Principle 3: Make Christ and salvation the central theme of every Bible study

Every Bible study subject that is presented should have Christ at the center. It is the Christ of the cross that attracts.

When individuals hear new truth, they may experience some tension when considering a change of lifestyle. But if they have committed their lives totally to Jesus, they will want to make a change. The goal in soul-winning work is to lead people to Jesus—to show them what He wants them to do.

> "Never should a sermon be preached, or Bible instruction in any line be given, without pointing the hearers to the Lamb of God that taketh away the sin of the world. (John 1:20) Every true doctrine makes Christ the center, every precept receives force from His words."
>
> *TESTIMONIES,* VOLUME 6, PAGE 54

Principle 4: Present text after text

The most effective and powerful Bible study presents one text upon another. Isaiah 28:10 teaches, "For precept must be upon precept, precept upon precept, line upon line, line upon line, here a little, there a little."

> "God designs that men shall not decide from impulse, but from weight of evidence, carefully comparing Scripture with Scripture."
>
> *DESIRE OF AGES*, PAGE 458

Some people find a Bible-marking guide helpful for those occasions when they are called upon to give spontaneous Bible studies. The texts can easily be found by marking your Bible through the **Bible Marking Plan**. The system is simple and easy to follow. Marking your Bible also helps you answer questions even if there were no lessons available. (See "Bible Marking Plan" in the appendix, Page 147)

Principle 5: Present testing truths after conversion

The more difficult testing-truth subjects should be presented after you have presented Jesus. When an individual experiences genuine conversion, his/her heart is open to receive more of God's truth.

> "You should not feel it your duty to introduce arguments upon the Sabbath question as you meet the people. If a person mentions the subject, tell them that this is not your burden now. But when they surrender heart and mind and will to God, they are then prepared candidly to weigh evidence in regard to these solemn, testing truths."
>
> *LETTER 77*, 1895

Principle 6: Keep your arguments to a few on any subject

It is best to use only a few texts and notes on any subject. Overload tends to make the mind weary.

> "It is not the best policy to be so very explicit, and say all upon a point that can be said, when a few arguments will cover the ground, and be sufficient for all practical purposes, to convince or silence opponents."
>
> *GOSPEL WORKERS*, PAGE 376

Principle 7: Answer questions

Encourage informal remarks and discussion. Answer questions from your students, but keep them on the subject you are studying. Honest questions, asked in a thoughtful way, may be cared for in the following ways:

- Answer completely at the time of the question.
- Promise to answer at the close of the study.
- Promise to answer completely in a future study more closely related to the question.

> "The best work you can do is to teach, to educate...sit down with some family, and let them ask questions. Then answer them patiently, humbly."
>
> *GOSPEL WORKERS,* PAGE 193

Principle 8: Give simple explanations

Keep your Bible Studies simple by giving simple explanations. It is very important to keep the study from getting too complicated. Use the lessons as they are. Simply read the questions then let the student read the text and answer the question. It is not necessary to a make a lot of extra comments.

> "Never search for words that will give the impression that you are learned. The greater your simplicity, the better will your words be understood."
>
> *GOSPEL WORKERS,* PAGE 89

Principle 9: Work with the love of God in your heart

Always show love toward the students you are studying with. People respond if they know you care about them.

> "The melting love of God in the hearts of the workers will be recognized by those for whom they labor... If you reveal the love of Christ to them, you may lead the hungering, thirsting ones to Jesus, and He will give them the bread of life and the waters of salvation."
>
> *LETTER 77,* 1895

Principle 10: Meet people where they are

It is important to meet people where they are. Every person is different. They are at different places in their spiritual experience. Consider the background of each of your Bible study contacts.

> "We also [like Christ] must learn to adapt our labors to the condition of the people—to meet men where they are. While the claims of the law of God are to be presented to the world, we should never forget that love—the love of Christ—is the only power that can soften the heart and lead to obedience."
>
> *EVANGELISM,* PAGE 57

Principle 11: Recount your own experience in conversion

Share your own testimony! **Tell what Jesus has done for you** in your life. This will be a blessing to those you are studying the Bible with.

> "**Tell** them how you found Jesus, and how blessed you have been since you gained an experience in His service. **Tell** them what blessing comes to you as you sit at the feet of Jesus, and learn precious lessons from His word. **Tell** them of the gladness and joy that there is in the Christian life. Your warm, fervent words will convince them that you have found the pearl of great price. Let your cheerful, encouraging words show that you have certainly found the higher way. This is genuine missionary work, and as it is done, many will awake as from a dream."
>
> *TESTIMONIES,* VOLUME 9, PAGE 38

Principle 12: Pray before each study

Prayer should always precede the opening of the Bible. A prayerful spirit makes all the difference. Go into the study with a humble, prayerful attitude.

> "Never should the Bible be studied without prayer. Before opening its pages we should ask for the enlightenment of the Holy Spirit, and it will be given."
>
> *STEPS TO CHRIST,* PAGE 91

Principle 13: Get decisions

Each lesson is designed with an opportunity at the end for the student to check for a decision. When you come to the end of each study, ask for a decision. It will then be easier when you come to difficult "testing truths" like the Sabbath, the true church, baptism, etc.

> "In every discourse fervent appeals should be made to the people to forsake their sins and turn to Christ."
>
> *TESTIMONIES,* VOLUME 4, PAGE 396

Remember Three Basic Important Concepts:

1. **Radiation** – Radiate the love of Jesus—His compassion and concern.
2. **Dedication** – Lead the student to dedicate his life to Jesus.
3. **Indoctrination** – Give the student a solid foundation in God's Holy word.

Depend on Christ—not on your own knowledge, wisdom or strength. Jesus says, "Without Me, you can do nothing." (John 15:5)

But He also says, "I can do all things through Christ who strengthens me." (Philippians 4:13)

CHAPTER 7

BEGINNING A BIBLE STUDY MINISTRY LET'S GET STARTED

God has given every Christian the wonderful privilege of sharing what Jesus has done for him or her. One of life's greatest joys is telling others about Jesus. God could have chosen sinless angels to carry the gospel to this rebellious planet. Instead, He chose us. What a privilege. What an opportunity. What a responsibility!

Although God has called every Christian to witness, He has especially called and gifted some to teach others His word in their homes. **These lay Bible teachers are an essential part of God's plan to reveal His truth to the world.**

Jesus' great commission to the Christian church is found at the close of the gospel of Matthew:

> "Go therefore and make disciples of all the nations, baptizing them in the name of the Father and of the Son and of the Holy Spirit, teaching them to observe all things that I have commanded you; and lo, I am with you always, even to the end of the age!"
>
> *MATTHEW 28:19-20*

Question 1: What action word describes Christ's command to His disciples? Matthew 28:19 (first word)

Answer:____

Jesus continually urges His disciples to go. **Go** is the little big word in the Bible. He tells His disciples "**Go** labor in my vineyard. **Go** compel them to come in. **Go** share the gospel." This "**Go**" comes echoing down the centuries urging us along with the New Testament disciples to **go** also.

Question 2: What three specific commands does Jesus' great commission include? Matthew 28:19-20

Answer: __________________________________

____

____

Teaching God's word is a vital part of God's plan. When we teach His word, disciples are made. When we teach His words, people accept Christ and His truth and are baptized. When we continue teaching His word after they are baptized, they continue to grow into strong, mature Christians. This is why Ellen White encourages us to:

> "Carry the word of God to every man's door, urge its plain statements upon every man's conscience, repeat to all the Savior's command, 'Search the Scriptures.'"
>
> *EVANGELISM*, PAGE 434

You can be part of God's exciting plan to finish His work. At the end of time, God will use humble lay people. The prophet of God witnessed a mighty lay movement in vision.

> "In visions of the night, representations passed before me of a great reformatory movement among God's people... Hundreds and thousands were seen visiting families, and opening before them the word of God...the world seemed to be lightened with the Heavenly influence."
>
> *TESTIMONIES*, VOLUME 9, PAGE 126

BASIC PLANS FOR GIVING BIBLE STUDIES

Here are some practical ways your church can get involved in fulfilling God's plan of carrying the gospel to the world through a lay-based Bible study ministry.

METHOD 1: BIBLE CORRESPONDENCE SCHOOL

Mail

The *Discover* Bible School can be used for people who would like to do their Bible lessons through correspondence. Through the years, thousands have been baptized as a result of the correspondence school.

Discover School - through *Voice Of Prophecy* central location
Discover School - through church-based location

Computer

The *It Is Written* website can be used for those who would like to do Bible lessons online.

It Is Written website- www.iiw.org

Two types of Bible correspondence schools

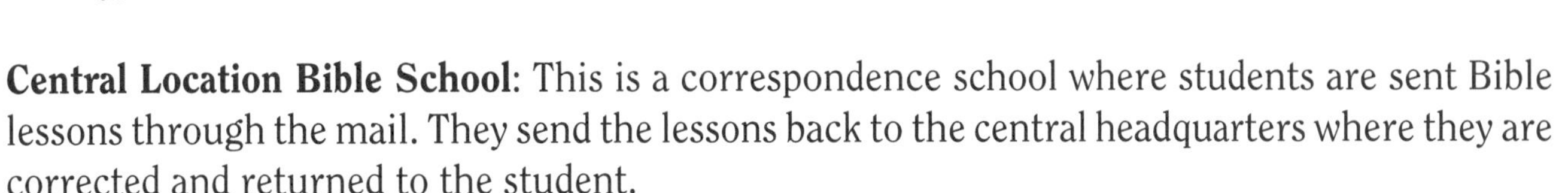

Central Location Bible School: This is a correspondence school where students are sent Bible lessons through the mail. They send the lessons back to the central headquarters where they are corrected and returned to the student.

Church-based Bible School: A church-based Bible school is led by a group of church members in a local church who have a vision to reach out to the people in their community and involve them in Bible study through correspondence. The church members accept the challenge and establish an organization to assist in accomplishing their vision. This Bible study outreach ministry is a called a Bible school.

Goals and purposes of a Bible school

- **Establish** redemptive friendships with Christians and the un-churched living in our communities.
- **Introduce** un-churched people to Jesus Christ and the Bible.
- **Acquaint** people with the teachings of the Bible.
- **Show** people how the Bible meets daily needs.
- **Help** students have a conversion experience as they study the Bible.
- **Assist** Christians in a continual understanding of the Bible and acquaint them with the Three Angels' Message.
- **Lead** students ultimately to a decision to be baptized and become part of God's remnant church.

How a *Discover* Bible School operates in the local church

Discover Bible lessons should be stocked at your local church.

Church members mail the lessons to the students. Each lesson is completed by the student and mailed back to the local church address. A church member then corrects the lesson and mails it back to the student, enclosing the next lesson.

One of the great values of establishing a *Discover* Bible School in your church is the number of church members who become involved. Some people have a desire to share their faith, but may be a little hesitant to meet with people in their homes.

Others who are computer literate can conduct Bible studies using the *Discover* lessons on the *It Is Written* website. Visitation teams can deliver books and answer questions by following up interests in their homes.

To begin a *Discover* Bible School in your church, please write to the following address:

Discover Bible School, 101 W. Cochran Street, Simi Valley, CA 93065

METHOD 2: PERSONAL BIBLE STUDIES IN THE HOME

One of the most spiritually-rewarding witnessing methods is giving personal Bible studies. Many church members who are hesitant at first, develop real skills in the art of studying the Bible with people in their home. In the process, these church members dramatically grow in both their knowledge of Jesus and the Bible.

Option 1: Giving personal Bible studies **using printed lessons**.

Soup & Salvation is the name of a weekly Bible study ministry class which follows up interests and gives Bible studies.

Giving personal Bible studies is so important there is a whole chapter written on it. (Further details, including a weekly schedule, are found in Chapter 9 - *Soup & Salvation*.)

Option 2: Giving Bible studies **using audiotapes, videotapes and digital video discs (DVD)**.

Hundreds of lay people are achieving new success in witnessing through Bible studies on audiotapes, videotapes and DVDs.

Friends and neighbors are invited to view one program per week. Each program is correlated with the *Search for Certainty* Bible lessons. This unique approach enables friends and neighbors to complete Bible lessons in the quietness of their own home without a Bible instructor.

The following are descriptions of the *Discoveries in Prophecy* and *Revelation of Hope* audio and video sets.

Discoveries in Prophecy and *Revelation of Hope* are full-message evangelistic campaigns available on tape—both audio and video. They are powerful resources for leading people into a dynamic relationship with the Lord Jesus Christ. Audio and videotape sets of the *Discoveries in Prophecy* or *Revelation of Hope* evangelistic series are available through *It Is Written*.

Whether used for **personal** spiritual growth, **small group Bible study** or a **public campaign**, Pastor Finley's riveting presentations on prophecy unlock the book of Revelation. With clarity, heartwarming illustrations and up-to-date applications, these Christ-centered prophetic messages are Mark Finley's evangelistic sermons, complete with graphics and appeals.

Pastors and lay people around the world are using these powerful audio and videotape presentations to win souls. *Discoveries in Prophecy* and the *Revelation of Hope* will touch hearts and change lives.

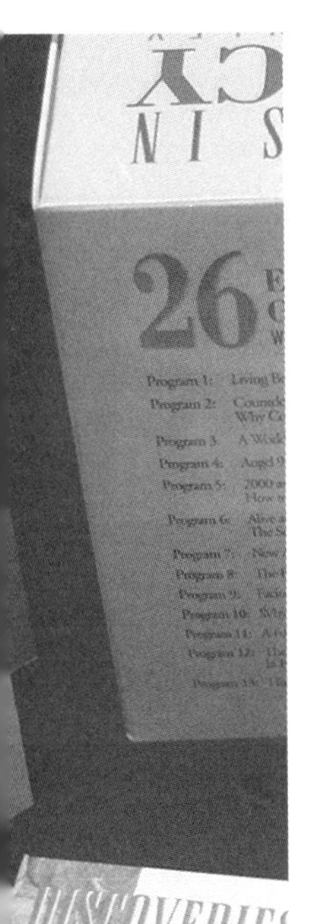

Following is a list of the 26 *Discoveries in Prophecy* sermons

Living Beyond 2000 *(Truthfulness of the Bible)*
Countdown to Eternity: Why Communism Failed *(Daniel 2)*
A World in Turmoil *(Matthew 24 or signs of the times)*
Angel 911: Revelation's Angelic Conflict *(Origin of evil)*
2000 and Beyond: How to Find Personal Peace *(Salvation)*
Alive at End Time: The Secret of Personal Power *(Divinity of Christ)*
New Age Conspiracy *(Manner of Christ's coming)*
The Beginning of the End *(The 2,300 days)*
Facing Revelation's Judgment *(The nature of the judgment)*
Why Our Streets Have Become Unsafe *(The Law)*
A 6,000 Year-Old Remedy for Tension *(Sabbath)*
The Greatest Religious Cover-up in History *(Change of Sabbath)*
How to Identify a Cult *(Discovering truth)*
The Coming Thousand Years: The Golden Age—or World Disaster? *(Millennium)*
The Real Truth About Near-Death Experiences *(State of the dead)*
How to Successfully Bury the Past *(Baptism)*
Will a Loving God Burn Sinners in Hell Forever? *(Hell)*
The Bible's Ancient Health Secrets Revealed *(Health)*
Why So Many Denominations? *(Four horsemen of Revelation)*
The Mystery of Revelation's Babylon Revealed *(Spiritual Babylon)*
The Search for Certainty *(True Church)*
A Financial Secret the World Doesn't Know *(Tithe)*
The Mark of the Beast *(Mark of the beast)*
The United States in Bible Prophecy *(When church and state unite)*
The Holy Spirit and the Unpardonable Sin *(Holy Spirit)*
Revelation's Glorious Climax *(Heaven)*

Following is a list of the 27 *Revelation of Hope* sermons

Revelation's Predictions for the New Millennium *(God's guidance into the future)*
Revelation's Greatest End-time Signs *(Matthew 24/Signs of the times)*
Revelation's Biggest Surprise *(Daniel 2/Prophecy of the future)*
Revelation's Star Wars – Battle Behind the Throne *(Origin of evil—Revelation 12)*
Revelation's Peacemaker *(Salvation/Jesus, Lamb of God)*
Revelation's Power Line – Secret of a Whole New Life *(God's power for deliverance)*
Revelation's Most Amazing Prophecy *(Introduction to Revelation)*
Revelation Reveals How Jesus Will Come *(Manner of Jesus' second coming)*
Revelation Predicts the Time of the End *(Judgment)*
Revelation's Answer to Crime, Lawlessness, Terrorism *(Law)*
Revelation's Eternal Sign *(The Sabbath)*
Revelation Exposes History's Greatest Hoax *(Change of the Sabbath)*
Revelation Unmasks the Cult Deception *(Dealing with deception)*
Revelation's Seven Last Plagues Unleashed *(Growth in Christian life)*
Revelation Reveals Deadly Delusions *(Spiritualism/State of the dead)*
Revelation's 1,000 Years of Peace *(Millennium/Revelation 20)*
Revelation's Lake of Fire *(Hell)*
Revelation's World of Tomorrow *(Heaven/Revelation 21-22)*
Revelation's New Life for a New Millennium *(Baptism—Washed in the blood of the Lamb)*
The Revelation Lifestyle *(Health/body temple)*
Revelation's Four Horsemen Galloping Across the Sky *(Why so many denominations?)*
Revelation's Last Appeal *(Mystery of spiritual Babylon revealed)*
Revelation's Mark of the Beast Exposed *(Mark of the beast)*
Revelation Describes the United States in Prophecy *(How the United States fits into prophecy)*
Revelation's Spiritual Revolution for a New Millennium *(The true church revealed)*
Revelation's Prophetic Movement at End Time *(The gift of prophecy)*
Revelation Reveals the Ultimate Answer to Life's Greatest Problems
(Revelation 10—God's prophetic movement)

New Beginnings, evangelistic sermons on DVD (digital video discs,) are a simple and interesting way to reach others with the gospel. You can either play it or preach it, and the programs can be used as Bible studies or even as evangelistic meetings. *It Is Written Television* has also developed the Evangelism Media Library, available on CD-ROM, which includes many new, exciting digital graphics which can be used by our ministers and laymen to illustrate Bible studies, seminars, sermons and evangelistic meetings.

Following is a list of the 26 *New Beginnings* sermons

How to Know the Future *(Daniel 2)*
Signs You Can't Ignore! *(Signs)*
The Great Escape *(Second coming)*
By Chance or Design? *(God of creation)*
Secrets of Ancient Scrolls *(Trust the Bible)*
Why So Much Suffering? *(Origin of sin)*
One Life Changed the World *(Who is Christ?)*
Born to Live Forever *(Salvation)*
Facing the Judgment with Confidence *(Judgment)*
What Happened to Right and Wrong? *(Law)*
Created for Something Better *(Sabbath)*
Millions Fooled by a Myth *(Change of the Sabbath)*
Turn Back the Clock *(Health)*
What Happens When You Die? *(Death)*
Evil in Chains *(Millennium)*
When the Smoke Clears *(Hell)*
Making a New Start *(Baptism)*
The Battle for the Throne *(Daniel 7)*
The Great Pretender *(Antichrist)*
Forever Marked *(Mark of the beast)*
Let Freedom Ring! *(United States in prophecy)*
Set Free by the Truth *(True church)*
Messages from Beyond the Stars *(Spirit of Prophecy)*
An Investment You Can't Lose *(Stewardship)*
Surviving the Coming Tribulation *(Seven last plagues)*
The Best is Yet to Come! *(Heaven)*

God has given man the wisdom to create exciting new technologies. While time lasts, **let's use every resource** at our command, every tool at our disposal, to win souls for His eternal kingdom!

CHAPTER 8

DEVELOPING YOUR BIBLE STUDY NOTEBOOK AND FILE BOX

Jesus often used simple methods to achieve unusual results. He multiplied five loaves and two fishes to feed over five thousand people. Five loaves and two fishes may not seem like much; but little in the hands of Jesus is much. When we use what we have, our Lord multiplies our efforts to accomplish marvelous things.

One of our Lord's great **soul-winning principles is to begin where you are with what you have**. If you do, God will surprise you. The principles in our lesson today may seem simple. They are. But follow these suggestions carefully and just watch what God does.

In this section, we will teach you how to develop a Bible study notebook. Your personal notebook will be an invaluable asset in teaching God's word to others.

A Bible study notebook and a file box of Bible study materials will become trusted resources that you will turn to repeatedly. In taking the time to develop a notebook and file box, we are laying the foundation of permanent success in our Bible study ministry.

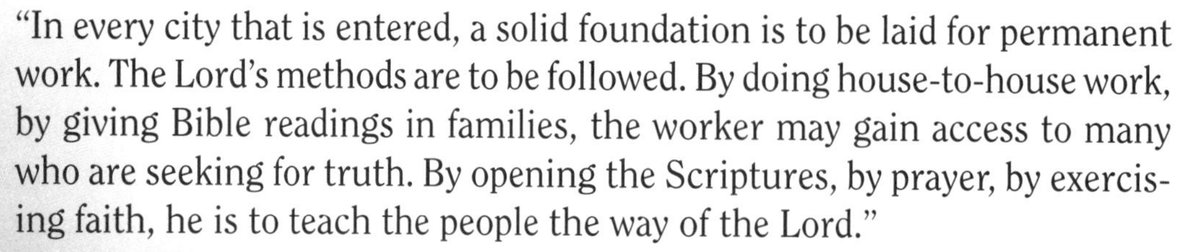

"In every city that is entered, a solid foundation is to be laid for permanent work. The Lord's methods are to be followed. By doing house-to-house work, by giving Bible readings in families, the worker may gain access to many who are seeking for truth. By opening the Scriptures, by prayer, by exercising faith, he is to teach the people the way of the Lord."

TESTIMONIES, VOLUME 7, PAGE 38

Decide what set of Bible study lessons to use

Using a printed series of Bible lessons has a least four decided advantages over simply opening your Bible and giving a Bible study.

1. The student does the lessons ahead of time, imprinting truth upon the mind.

2. Reading the question and writing in the answer provides a double impact. Truth is more firmly fixed in the mind.

3. Hearing the lesson presented by the instructor provides a third opportunity for the interested person to grasp truth.

4. Students can return to their lessons repeatedly to review the truths they have learned.

***Search for Certainty* Bible Lessons**

The *Search for Certainty* Bible lessons are a complete set of Christ-centered, prophetic, doctrinal studies. Each lesson covers a Bible topic. Each lesson is designed to build on the next one. Study each lesson yourself. It's difficult to teach others without knowing the lesson well yourself.

- Get a small notebook for all your Bible lessons. Place each lesson in the notebook.
- Complete each lesson.
- Take your master notebook of lessons and your Bible with you when you go into a home.

*Note: If you need extra help in answering questions or finding texts, the book *Studying Together* by Mark Finley is very helpful.

"**It is a sin for those who attempt to teach the word to others to be themselves neglectful of its study**... The life of God, which gives life to the world, is in His word. It was by His word that Jesus healed disease and cast out demons. By His word He stilled the sea and raised the dead; and the people bore witness that His word was with power. He spoke the word of God as He had spoken it to all the Old Testament writers. The whole Bible is a manifestation of Christ. It is our only source of power."

GOSPEL WORKERS, PAGES 249-250

1. Purchase a file box and file folders
2. Set up file folders for each of the lessons
3. Set up file folders for materials such as:
    - Registration forms
    - *It Is Written Television* and *Voice of Prophecy* station logs listing the time and location of the broadcast
    - *Search for Certainty*, *Discover* or *Something Wonderful* Bible enrollment cards
    - Brochures of any seminars, health programs or evangelistic meetings
    - Small books or literature on salvation, the second coming, the Sabbath, the state of the dead, the true church, etc.
    - Alphabetical file for all registered Bible students (All Bible study registration forms are filed here.)

PLOTTING NAMES

Plotting names ahead of time is extremely important. We will be more effective and use time more efficiently if all the names for visitation are located on a map ahead of time. Before you begin your visitation, spend a few minutes finding each address on a map. Plan your visitation strategy to visit homes located nearest one another first; then proceed to homes further away.

As society becomes increasingly more mobile, it is difficult to find people at home. Often it is necessary to return to the same home many times.

During one evangelistic series in a major New England city, one of our lay Bible instructors visited a home six times before he found the lady home. When he did, he found she was extremely interested. He began giving her Bible studies. Persistence in visitation pays off. Look at it this way: Even if no one is there, at least you have located the home for a future visit.

> "This house-to-house labor, searching for souls, hunting for the lost sheep, is the most essential work that can be done."
>
> *EVANGELISM*, PAGE 431

Materials Needed To Successfully Conduct Bible Studies

Churches with successful Bible schools or Bible study ministries select a Bible study coordinator. The Bible study interest coordinator prepares the essential materials for the Bible study ministry outreach.

Here is what you will need:

Maps of your community

- Each team of two people needs a map.

Names and addresses

- Get names and addresses of all interests from every source.
- Prepare a visitation card for each one.

Bible study enrollment cards

- These cards can be mass-mailed or hand-distributed.
- Compile the *Search for Certainty, Something Wonderful, Prophecy* or *Discover* response cards.
- Sort all names by zip codes.
- Code each interest on the interest card.
- Organize your visitation by areas.
- Be sure to make a master copy of all your interests. Since each visitation team will take the interest cards they have received with them, your master list will ensure you do not misplace names. The master list is vital for future contacts and mailings.

• The coordinator will keep track of all the interests
• The coordinator will develop a master notebook, with a record of all the Bible instructors' studies. This record can be updated to show the progress of each student indicating the number of studies he or she has completed.

Bibles
• Some individuals you visit may not have their own Bible; therefore, it is important to provide each student with a copy of the Scriptures.

Bible study registration forms (See appendix Page 148)
• Every person who begins Bible studies is enrolled using the Bible study registration form. This is an excellent way to keep track of their lesson progress.

Bible study lessons
• *Search for Certainty* Bible study lessons—designed specifically for in-home Bible studies with lay Bible teachers.
• *Discover* Bible lessons—designed specifically as correspondence lessons.

Bible handbook *Studying Together*
• *Studying Together* by Mark Finley is a Bible handbook that will be helpful in answering questions and objections.

Books and literature for visitation
• Select literature on salvation, the second coming, the Sabbath, etc.

We recommend:
• *Steps to Christ*
—to lead people into a closer walk with God.
• *The Almost Forgotten Day*
—on the Bible Sabbath.
• *Why So Many Denominations?*
—about the true church throughout history.
• *Revelation's Predictions for a New Millennium*
—a book of all the major doctrines in Scripture.

Note: These books are available at your local Adventist Book Center (ABC).

Baptismal manual
The baptismal manual reviews all major doctrinal truths in preparation for baptism. (available at your local ABC)

When we prepare thoroughly, organize efficiently and plan systematically, God can do much more through us. Organization does not substitute for the power of the Holy Spirit, but it does create opportunities for the Holy Spirit to work more powerfully.

Organization also sends a signal to the entire church; soul-winning is important. If corporate executives put together comprehensive organized strategies to ensure larger corporate profits, shouldn't the church thoroughly organize to advance the kingdom of God?

It may take time. It will take effort. But your church will reap rich dividends. People won for the kingdom are well worth it.

Yes! You are ready to begin giving Bible studies

You have now completed all the Bible lessons. You have them in a notebook. You have your Bible study file box established. You have filled out the Bible study registration form for each student. You are ready to begin.

Start by giving your first series of Bible studies to a friend, relative, neighbor or co-worker. Tell them about the classes you have been attending. Ask them if you can practice by giving the lessons to them.

How to Give the Bible Study

Be sure the Bible student has received Lesson 1.

The instructor

- Offers a short prayer.
- Goes through the Bible lesson just as it is.
- Reads the notes and the questions.

The student

- Reads the Bible text and answers the questions.

The instructor

- Asks the decision question after each lesson.
- Asks if they have any questions.
- Asks if the lesson was clear.
- Gives the student the next lesson.
- Asks if they could have a simple prayer of thanks.
- Engages in a short personal conversation with the student.
- Says good-bye.

Helpful suggestions for giving Bible studies

Pray with your students before each study

A prayerful spirit makes all the difference. Go into the study with a humble attitude.

Keep the Bible study simple

It is important to keep the study from getting too complicated. Use the lessons as they are. Simply read the questions then let the student read the text and answer the question. Extra comments should be minimized.

Keep the Bible study short and to the point

Each Bible study should last only about 45-50 minutes. You should not spend more than one hour on any lesson. Stay on the topic. Do not wander away from the lesson. When questions come up that are on a different subject, respond by saying something like this, "Next week we cover that subject in detail. Could we address your question then? That will enable us to stay right on the point of our lesson today."

Be a learner

Don't claim to be an authority on the Bible. It is important not to give your students the impression that you think you have all the answers and they don't know anything.

Study the lessons in the order given

These lessons have been written in such a way as to lay a foundation for the more difficult subjects coming in the future. Follow the lessons in the order given. Your students will comprehend the Bible much more easily.

Be consistent

Consistency is very important. Study every week at the same time. Your students will look forward to this special time set aside for Bible study.

Study one lesson at a time, two at the most

Your student may feel overwhelmed if you try to study too many lessons. One at a time is probably best; however, there may be times when a student can do two lessons at a time very successfully.

Let the student ask questions

Questions will arise that you may not be prepared to answer. Don't pretend you know the answer. If you don't know the answer to a question, tell them you don't know. Say, "I'm not sure about the answer, but I will find out and give you an answer next week."

Keep the student on track

Keep the student on the lesson you are studying, not several different subjects. When a student asks questions on another subject, try to bring them back to the subject you are studying.

Ask for a decision at the end of each lesson

Each lesson is designed with an opportunity at the end for the student to indicate a decision. When you come to the end of each lesson, ask for a decision.

Depend on Christ

Do not depend on your own knowledge or strength. Jesus says, "Without Me, you can do nothing." (John 15:5)

REMEMBER THIS SPECIAL PROMISE

"He who **begins with a little knowledge**, in a humble way, and tells what he knows, while seeking diligently for further knowledge, will find the whole heavenly treasure awaiting his demand. The more he seeks to impart light, the more light he will receive. The more one tries to explain the word of God to others, with a love for souls, the plainer it becomes to himself. The more we use our knowledge and exercise our powers, the more knowledge and power we shall have."

CHRIST'S OBJECT LESSONS, PAGE 354

To succeed in this kind of work we must have the power and presence of the Holy Spirit.

CHAPTER 9

Soup & Salvation

AN ORGANIZED BIBLE STUDY PROGRAM

Have you ever wondered why many churches have little interest in witnessing? Have you ever asked, "Is there something our church can do to make a difference for the kingdom of God in our community? How can we have a real breakthrough in outreach?" Many concerned church members have asked these questions. Jesus provides us with some answers.

When our Lord called His disciples He said, "Follow Me and I will make you fishers of men." (Matthew 4:19) The disciples learned to be effective soul-winners as they watched Jesus share eternal truths with lost people. Spending time with Jesus, they learned how to win souls. After they were with Him only a very short time, Jesus sent them out as soul-winners. The disciples applied what Jesus had taught them.

You cannot learn to swim in a classroom. It is necessary to get in the water. You cannot learn soul-winning in a classroom either. You learn soul-winning by going into the field. We step out in faith. The Holy Spirit teaches us how to be more effective. When we share what we know, we grow.

In this session we will share a simple soul-winning strategy that is revolutionizing churches. It is called *Soup & Salvation*. *Soup & Salvation* is a weekly Bible study program designed to follow up interests and give Bible studies.

Beginning personal Bible studies through *Soup & Salvation*

Let's begin by answering a few basic questions you may have about how to organize *Soup & Salvation*.

When is a good time to begin *Soup & Salvation* and how long does it last?

Soup & Salvation begins approximately 10-12 weeks after the series of *Lighting Your World for God* training classes are over. (This gives the Bible instructors enough time to give some practice Bible studies.) Lay Bible instructors are encouraged to complete the *Search for Certainty* lessons themselves, place them in a notebook, develop a file box and give some "practice" Bible studies before following up the interests generated from the mass mailing cards prepared for *Soup & Salvation*.

Soup & Salvation is scheduled after the mass mailing of the Bible study enrollment cards. It should be timed so the request cards for Bible studies come in approximately a week before the program begins.

What time is the program conducted?

Soup & Salvation is conducted once a week in the evening from 6:00 p.m. to 9:00 p.m., or on Sabbath afternoon from 2:00 p.m. to 5:00 p.m.

How long does the program last?

Soup & Salvation is usually conducted for about 12 weeks. This gives lay people the opportunity to establish regular Bible studies.

How is *Soup & Salvation* conducted?

Church members choose to participate in one of four core soul-winning ministries.

1. Prayer ministry
2. Literature ministry
3. Visitation ministry
4. Bible study ministry

Each ministry focuses on a specific area. Members with similar gifts and interests join together in a specific outreach ministry at each session.

When a significant number of church members meet together on the same evening to pray, visit, distribute literature or give Bible studies, the Holy Spirit acknowledges their commitment by empowering their efforts for service.

Let's examine how each group functions. We begin with the prayer ministry group.

MINISTRY 1 — PRAYER

Question 1: What instruction does our Lord give us through the heart-cry of Job? Job 16:21

Answer: ____

____

Intercession is pleading with God for other people. The prayer ministry group spends time in earnest prayer regarding the salvation of specific people. The prayer ministry group prays when the Bible study ministry group is giving Bible studies, the visitation group is visiting and the literature group is distributing Bible enrollment cards. The prayer ministry group prays by name for both the visitors and the interests.

Question 2: At a time of apostasy in Israel, what words of encouragement did the prophet Samuel give? I Samuel 12:22

Answer: ____

____

The prophet Samuel was hopeful God would bring a powerful revival to His people. He prayed that he would not sin against the Lord by ceasing to pray for spiritually-needy Israel. Again in our day, God appeals for committed church members to become involved in intercession.

Question 3: What commitment did Samuel make to Israel? I Samuel 12:23

Answer: ____

____

Samuel made a commitment to seek God on Israel's behalf. In our prayer ministry group, we pray for people who may not be praying for themselves. We intercede for the lost. We seek God recognizing that only He can transform hearts and change lives.

> "Why do not believers feel a deeper, more earnest concern for those who are out of Christ? Why do not two or three meet together and plead with God for the salvation of some special one, and then for still another? In our churches let companies be formed for service. Let different ones unite in labor as fishers of men."
>
> *TESTIMONIES*, VOLUME 7, PAGE 21

What does the prayer ministry team do at the *Soup & Salvation* program?

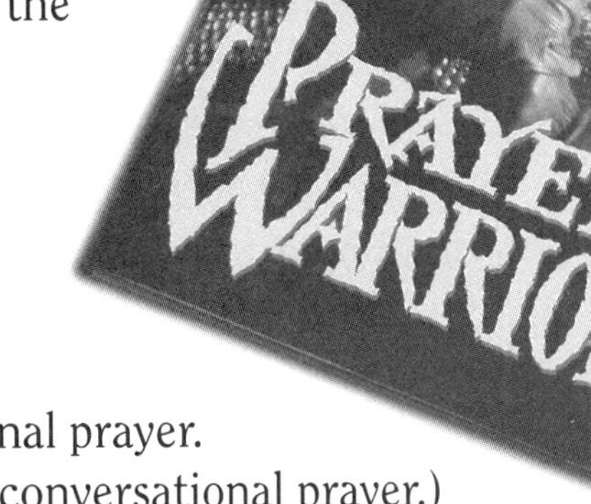

• Study *Prayer Warriors* – We suggest a brief study on intercessory prayer using pastor Ron Halvorsen's *Prayer Warriors*. The *Prayer Warriors* manual presents 13 lessons on the power of intercession. It presents the power of prayer in the battle between good and evil.
• Study the Bible (Acts) – You may also desire to use the book of Acts as a background for your prayer ministry group. Read five to ten verses. Make a few brief comments, enlist group members in a discussion on the Holy Spirit and then spend the rest of your time in prayer.
• Pray for approximately 45-50 minutes.
• Pray specifically for Bible study contacts.
• Pray for the lay Bible instructors following up Bible study contacts.
• Talk to God as to a friend by using conversational prayer.
(See appendix Page 134 for an entire section on conversational prayer.)

Getting started in prayer ministry:
• Choose a prayer ministry coordinator.
• Ask specific people to join your group. The prayer ministry group is made up of church members with the God-given burden of intercession.
• Commit to meet once a week at *Soup & Salvation*.
• Pray for specific names of those being visited and for the visitor.

MINISTRY 2 — VISITATION

The members in visitation ministry visit those on the pastor's interest list. The pastor's current interest list should include interests resulting from media programs, health program contacts, contacts from former evangelistic meetings, previous Bible study contacts, former or inactive Adventists and anyone else the pastor may have on his/her interest list.

> "If the teachers of the word are willing, the Lord will lead them into close relation with the people. He will guide them to the homes of those who need and desire the truth; and as the servants of God engage in the work of seeking for the lost sheep, their spiritual faculties are awakened and energized."
>
> *EVANGELISM*, PAGE 463

Getting started in visitation ministry:

- **Choose** a visitation coordinator.
- **Organize** your visitation team.
- **Commit** to attend *Soup & Salvation* once per week.
- **Visit** people on the pastor's current interest list.

Purpose: The specific purpose of this group is to develop relationships by sharing appropriate literature. Lives are changed as they study the word of God, so the ultimate purpose is to get individuals enrolled in the *Search for Certainty* Bible study lessons. Literature we recommend for visitation:

The *Search for Certainty* Bible study enrollment card and Bible lessons
Peace Above the Storm
Satisfied (2003 sharing book)

Sample visits: See Page 137 for sample visits.

MINISTRY 3 — LITERATURE

There are many church members who will get involved in literature ministry. This is a way to bring the message of God to everyone's door.

Literature is a vital part of God's plan for saving thousands. On numerous occasions, people have found old pieces of discarded literature. They have read eagerly and God has used it to change their lives. A piece of literature can be read over and over again. It can be passed on for years from one person to the next. We have a responsibility to take tracts, pamphlets and books to people everywhere around the world.

Look at these insightful statements in the book *Evangelism* by Ellen White:

> "The press is a powerful means to move the minds and hearts of the people. The men of this world seize the press, and make the most of every opportunity to get poisonous literature before the people. If men, under the influence of the spirit of the world and of Satan, are earnest to circulate books, tracts and papers of a corrupting nature, you should be more earnest to get reading matter of an elevating and saving character before the people. Tracts, papers and books, as the case demands, should be circulated in all the cities and villages in the land."
>
> *EVANGELISM*, PAGES 160-161

> "Publications must be multiplied, and scattered like the leaves of autumn. These silent messengers are enlightening and molding the minds of thousands in every country and in every clime."
>
> *COLPORTEUR MINISTRY*, PAGE 5

Question 4: What specific instruction did the Lord give Habakkuk? Habakkuk 2:2-3

Answer: ______________________________________

God instructed the prophet Habakkuk to write the vision so future generations could be blessed. Literature ministry expands the influence of God's word. It has the potential to impact multitudes.

The purpose of literature ministry is to:

- Distribute literature and tracts
- Distribute Bible enrollment cards
- Distribute *Something Wonderful* and *Search for Certainty* Bible enrollment cards
- Begin systematic mailings—begin mailing letters that will cultivate casual contacts into systematic Bible studies
- Conduct door-to-door surveys (See Page 137)

Regular mailings to names in the interest file can produce a 25 percent response over the period of one year if the mailings are varied.

It is beneficial to mail once a quarter to the interest file list.

Here are four different types of mailings we suggest

1. **An invitation** to begin Bible studies
2. **A free book** offer
3. **An invitation** to one of our seminars—either *Natural Lifestyle Cooking, Unsealing Daniel's Mysteries* or *Discover Jesus*
4. **An invitation** to the *Discoveries in Prophecy*, *Revelation of Hope* or *New Beginnings* evangelistic meetings

We have included four sample letters in this manual. You can adapt them to meet your own needs. (See Pages 127-130)

Getting started in literature ministry:
- Choose a literature ministry coordinator.
- The coordinator selects at least five people to join the group.
- Commit to attend *Soup & Salvation* once per week for 12 weeks, distributing or mailing literature.
- Organize teams – go out by twos.
- Organize territory – acquire maps, allowing one map for each two teams. Two teams can work on the same street or in the same area. Mount a master map on a board.
- Use markers – color-code literature distribution yellow and door-to-door surveys green.
- Choose appropriate Bible study interest cards, advertising materials and truth-filled literature.
- Go out, distributing literature, tracts, Bible enrollment cards, selling books and literature or conducting door-to-door surveys.

MINISTRY 4 — BIBLE STUDY

All the participants from the *Lighting Your World For God* training classes are the core group for *Soup & Salvation*. They meet once a week for 12 weeks for approximately three hours, including a light meal. Each participant visits the homes of those requesting Bible studies. After finding people to study the Bible with, Bible studies are continued weekly.

There are people in your community who are waiting for someone to come to their home and study the Bible with them.

Question 5: When Philip asked the Ethiopian if he understood the portion of Scripture he was reading, how did the man respond? Acts 8:31

Answer: ____

Question 6: What did Philip do? Acts 8:35

Answer: ____

God providentially led Philip to the Ethiopian, just like He did Peter to Cornelius. The Ethiopian was confused in his understanding of Scripture. Philip carefully explained the truth of God's word. God will lead you to truth-seekers as well.

> "All over the world men and women are looking wistfully to heaven. Prayers and tears and inquiries go up from souls longing for light, for grace, for the Holy Spirit. Many are on the verge of the kingdom, waiting only to be gathered in."
>
> *ACTS OF THE APOSTLES*, PAGE 109

What do the participants in the Bible study ministry do?

- They follow up the *Search for Certainty*, *Prophecy* or *Discover* Bible enrollment cards.
- They give the Bible studies each week.

> "The Lord's methods are to be followed. By doing house-to-house work, by giving Bible reading in families, the worker may gain access to many who are seeking for truth. By opening the Scriptures, by prayer, by exercising faith, he is to teach the people the way of the Lord."
>
> *TESTIMONIES*, VOLUME 7, PAGE 38

Getting started in Bible study ministry:

- **Choose** a Bible study ministry coordinator.
- **Commit** to attend *Soup & Salvation* once per week for 12 weeks, dedicating one evening or afternoon per week to giving Bible studies.
- **Organize** materials—maps, Bibles, *Search For Certainty* Bible lessons and Bible enrollment cards.
- **Give** at least one Bible study every week.

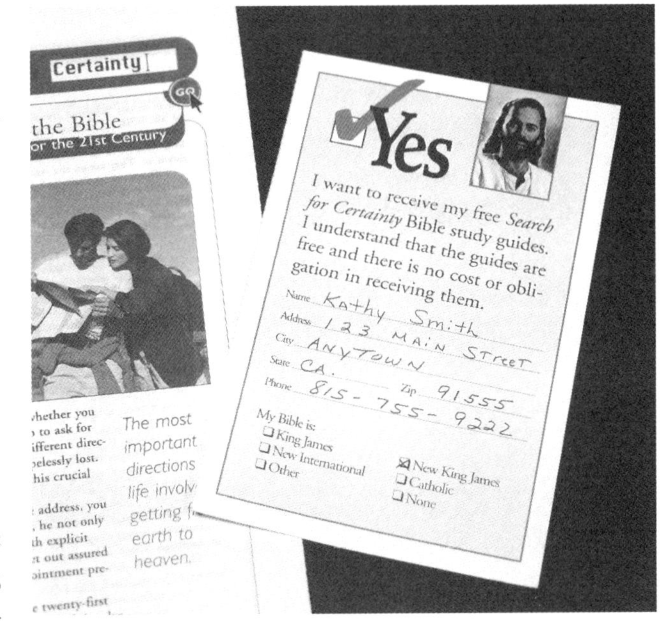

How can you reap a large harvest from your Bible study interests?

The key is to follow up each Bible study with some kind of evangelistic reaping series. Reaping meetings can take a variety of forms including: an evangelist preaching, a pastor or lay member preaching, or through the use of multimedia visuals. More people are becoming actively involved in evangelistic meetings today using video series such as *Discoveries in Prophecy* or *Revelation of Hope*. In addition, thousands of lay people are using the *New Beginnings* digital video discs.

Church members invite Bible study interests to the evangelistic meetings, which can be conducted in a home, hotel meeting room or church.

Public evangelistic meetings will reinforce the truths your students learned in the Bible studies. These reaping meetings will solidify their interest and lead them to a decision for Christ and His truth.

IMAGINE THIS SCENE!

- The lights are on at your church on Tuesday evening. The parking lot is jammed. Church members are gathering for an evening of witness.
- Prayer groups are scattered throughout the church. People are on their knees seeking God. Earnest, heart-felt prayers of intercession for the lost ascend to God's throne.
- Visitation teams leave the church to visit former Adventists and encourage them to return to church.
- Parents and children are distributing literature in the area around the church.
- Pastors and lay people are giving Bible studies to hundreds.
- The Holy Spirit is poured out. Revival fires are kindled. The church is ablaze with the glory of God.

This can be a picture of your church. May it be so! In the kingdom of God someone will come up to you and say, "Thank you for giving me that Bible study. Because of you, hallelujah, I have found Him!"

CHAPTER 10

DEALING WITH OBJECTIONS

Jesus was a master at answering questions. When a scribe asked a potentially volatile question regarding the greatest commandment in the law, Jesus gave a classic answer in Mark 12:30-31— "Love God with all your heart and love your neighbor as yourself." What many Christians do not realize is this: Jesus was quoting from the Old Testament. "Love God with all your heart" is a direct quote from Deuteronomy 6:5. His answer, "Love your neighbor as yourself," is a quote from Leviticus 19:18.

Jesus filled His mind with passages of Scripture. He was thoroughly acquainted with God's word. **The Savior patiently listened to people's questions and kindly answered them from God's word.**

When you are giving a series of Bible studies, people will raise questions regarding the new truths they are learning. Sometimes their objections may be extremely strong. This does not mean they are not interested. It may mean the Holy Spirit is deeply convicting them and they are confused.

- **Deal** with them **kindly**, lovingly and positively
- **Listen** to their objections
- **Seek God** for wisdom
- **Answer their questions** from the Bible

Very few people make up their minds to accept truth and unite with the church without a struggle.

Their decision will have personal, economic and social consequences. They need help to decide correctly. They are constantly considering the consequences they may experience if they do what Jesus wants them to do.

Since they must make a personal evaluation of these consequences, only they know what is really hindering them. Some hindrances are very real. For this reason, the soul-winner should welcome objections as a wonderful opportunity to help the individual to complete surrender to God and His truth.

DISCOVERING THE OBSTACLES OR PROBLEMS

POINT 1 – DISCOVER WHAT HINDERS THEM

If you do not know what is holding a person back from accepting Christ, keeping the Sabbath, attending church, being baptized, etc., you can give Bible studies endlessly and never lead the person to take his stand and unite with the family of God. You must first discover the obstacle, then find a way to help the person reach out in faith to the God who can solve the problem.

As you ask your Bible student questions, you will discover what is holding him/her back from making a decision for Christ. You cannot help a person fully surrender to Jesus if you do not know what is keeping him/her from doing so. You cannot help a person overcome obstacles if you don't know what they are.

Question 1: What significant question did Ananias ask the Apostle Paul regarding a decision for baptism? Acts 22:16

Answer: ______________________________

____

Question 2: What important question did the Apostle Paul ask King Agrippa? Acts 26:27 (first part)

Answer: ______________________________

____

The important questions to ask are,
"Why are you waiting—do you believe? God wants you to move ahead."

> "The sacred responsibility rests upon the minister to watch for souls as one that must give an account. He must interest himself in the souls for whom he labors, finding out all that perplexes and troubles them and hinders them from walking in the light of the truth."
>
> *REVIEW AND HERALD*, AUGUST 30, 1892

Here are some practical, sample decision questions you can ask on a few key topics:

SALVATION
- ❑ Have you ever previously committed your life to Jesus?
- ❑ Would you like to accept Jesus' offer of eternal life right now?
- ❑ Is there anything that might hinder you?

SABBATH
- ❑ Is the Sabbath new to you?
- ❑ Do you have any questions on the Bible Sabbath?
- ❑ Is there anything that would hinder you from keeping the Sabbath?

BAPTISM
- ❑ Do you understand Bible baptism is by immersion?
- ❑ Have you ever thought about being baptized?
- ❑ What might hinder you from moving ahead in baptism?

POINT 2 – COME CLOSE TO YOUR BIBLE STUDY CONTACTS

Getting close to your Bible study contacts will help them through the difficult time of meeting obstacles.

Question 3: What statements did Jesus use to break down prejudice and win the hearts of the following people?

The Centurion – Matthew 8:10

Answer: ______________________________

The Canaanite woman – Matthew 15:28

Answer: ______________________________

Jesus reaffirmed the faith of the Centurion and the Canaanite woman. He said, "I have not seen such great faith," and "Great is your faith." Come close to your Bible study contact and reaffirm their faith.

> "Many a laborer fails in his work because he does not come close to those who most need his help. With the Bible in hand, he should seek in a courteous manner to learn the objections which exist in the minds of those who are beginning to inquire, 'What is truth?' Carefully and tenderly should he lead and educate them, as pupils in a school."
>
> *GOSPEL WORKERS*, PAGE 190

By coming close to people, you will win their confidence. They will feel safe in expressing their feelings and problems to you. **Encourage a give-and-take dialogue. Listen** to what the they are saying. Encourage them to express their opinions on the topic being discussed. Even if their ideas are far-fetched, listen kindly and ask tactful questions.

You might say, **"That is an interesting thought. In our Bible study I am sure this topic will become clearer."**

This puts you in a different light; it isn't you on one side and the person on the other. You are asking God for answers together.

POINT 3 – NEVER ARGUE

If the person says he does not agree with some point of truth, you might say: "I'm glad you have expressed yourself. Let's discuss the area you have questions in. I am thankful the Bible has the answers."

Never argue—you may win the argument, but lose an interest. Dwell on the affirmative, not the negative points.

> "Often, as you seek to present the truth, opposition will be aroused; but if you seek to meet the opposition with an argument you will only multiply it, and that you cannot afford to do. Hold to the affirmative. Angels of God are watching you, and they understand how to impress those whose opposition you refuse to meet with argument."
>
> *TESTIMONIES*, VOLUME 9, PAGES 147-148

We strengthen arguments when we repeat them. Stay always to the affirmative. Don't spend a lot of time discussing objections. Carefully consider the objection, then suggest prayer for wisdom.

You could say something like this: "I'm glad you told me how you feel about this. It is important to you, and I believe the Lord has the answer. Let's ask Him to help us."

Then just offer a short prayer asking God to give an answer to the problem. Then meet the problem or objection with texts, if appropriate for the solution.

POINT 4 – AVOID CONFLICT

The natural tendency is to meet an objection head-on, defending ourselves and attacking the questioner. Avoid at all costs the atmosphere of conflict, giving the individual the impression you desire to prove him or her wrong.

POINT 5 – EXPECT OBJECTIONS, DON'T BE SURPRISED BY THEM

It is important to expect objections from your Bible student. Don't be surprised or overwhelmed by them. Whenever you present anything new or different to people, they will have questions. People will often challenge the new and untried. Be patient with them. Create an affirming atmosphere. Welcome questions and objections gracefully.

When people have objections, what might this indicate?

- ❏ The person has genuine questions that loom large in his/her mind.
- ❏ The person has not yet fully made up his/her mind on the topic.
- ❏ The person may be using an objection to defend himself/herself.

Effective ways to answer objections

1. USE THE F-F-F PRINCIPLE

F = Feel – "Mr. ____, I understand how you feel."
People want to know that you understand their feelings. They don't want to feel odd or strange when they express themselves.

F = Felt – "Many others in your present situation have felt exactly the same way."
People also want to know they are not alone with their question or in their feelings. You may want to briefly tell a story or use an example of how you or someone close to you had the same questions.

F = Found – "But, Mr. _____, others have found..."
Share concrete, practical solutions others have found.

2. ANSWER OBJECTIONS BEFORE THEY ARE RAISED

Once an individual has made a statement or offered an objection, he likes to defend that point.

One of the best ways to answer those objections is by posing a question and then answering it with Scripture.

The *Search for Certainty* Bible lessons do this throughout the series.

3. GIVE SHORT, CONCISE ANSWERS

❑ Ask if the answer clears up the issue.

4. LISTEN CAREFULLY TO EACH OBJECTION

❑ Make sure they have an objection, and not an excuse, by asking if that is their only reason for not deciding.

❑ Ask, "If this issue was cleared up, would you then see your way clear to accept Christ [keep the Sabbath, be baptized, etc.]? Is this the only thing holding you back?"

❑ Show the person you understand the objection by repeating it in your own words. Example: "Do I understand that the issue really holding you back is your husband's opposition? Or are you worried that Sabbath-keeping will cause you to lose your job?"

❑ Get a commitment that, if the objection could be removed, he or she would make a decision immediately.

❑ Answer the objection. Use a few well-chosen Bible texts.

❑ Invite decision. Ask the person for a decision on the topic. If they are hesitant, pray about it with them.

5. MEET OBJECTIONS WITH TEXTS

It isn't possible to know beforehand what particular objection, excuse or hindrance to decision you will have to meet. Here are a few common ones on keeping the Sabbath:

Regarding their job

"I'll lose my job."
"I can't support my family if I don't work on Saturday."
"I can't find another job."

Texts

Matthew 6:30-33

Psalm 37:3

Isaiah 65:13-14

Isaiah 1:19-20

Regarding their business

"Saturday is my best day for business."
"My business will be ruined if I close Saturdays."
"I'm in debt, I need all the money I can make."
"I'll never get ahead in the business world."

Texts

Matthew 16:26

Mark 8:35

John 6:27

Isaiah 56:2-5

Luke 12:19-20

Regarding the Sabbath

"It's so inconvenient to keep a different day."
"I'll be out of step with the rest of the world."
"So few keep Saturday; the majority keep Sunday."

Texts

Galatians 1:10

John 15:14

Luke 6:22-23,26

Proverbs 29:25

Philippians 3:8

Matthew 10:37

John 15:19

Miscellaneous objections regarding the Sabbath

"Sunday was good enough for my father and all my ancestors, shouldn't it be good enough for me?"

"I've kept Sunday all my life, why is God calling me now to keep the Sabbath?"

Texts
Acts 17:30
John 9:41
Ezekiel 18:20
John 21:22

The Holy Spirit will lead you to give the right answers to the questions you are asked. Sometimes you will be amazed at what comes out of your mouth. You will give answers that you did not realize you could give. Texts you have stored in your mind will be brought to your memory. Truths you have learned through the years will come back to your mind. God will give you answers.

POINT 6 – KEEP YOUR HEART UPLIFTED IN PRAYER

It is critically important to uplift your heart in prayer. Ask God to give you wisdom as you study His word with your Bible students. He will give you the right words to say.

> "If the worker keeps his heart uplifted in prayer, God will help him to speak the right word at the right time."
>
> *GOSPEL WORKERS*, PAGE 120

- God will give you wisdom. He will give you souls for His kingdom.
- Soul-winning is not our work, it is God's work.
- Winning people for the kingdom is not our task, it is His. We are His instruments.
- Allow God to use you and you will be amazed at what He does.
- In Christ, you are wiser than you know.

CHAPTER 11

YOU CAN GAIN DECISIONS

A young evangelist wanted to learn how to be successful in leading people to a decision for Christ. He asked the great, experienced evangelist, Robert Boothby, how he got so many decisions in his work of soul-winning. Pastor Boothby replied, **"You don't expect to get decisions every time you preach, do you?"**

"Oh no," the young evangelist answered, "not every time, but I do expect to get decisions some of the time."

As quick as a flash, Boothby answered, "That is precisely your problem, young man. You must expect to get decisions every time you preach. Then you will get them."

This principle applies for Bible studies as well as evangelistic sermons. If we do not expect people to make decisions on the topic we are presenting, generally they will not. Major life decisions are normally made incrementally. You are what you are today because of the decisions or choices you have made all of your life. Some of these choices were very large. Others were very small. The sum of those decisions determined the direction of your life.

People rarely make a huge leap to accept the total body of God's truth all at once. They accept it a step at a time. Generally there are **four steps people take in making decisions**.

1. The **information** must be clear. Their questions must be answered.

2. They must feel a **conviction** this is what God wants them to do.

3. They must have a **desire** to do it.

4. They must take **action**.

FOUR LEVELS OF DECISION

In dealing with a person making a decision in any area of life, there are four basic levels of decision to be considered. In this lesson we will study how to help people take these four steps.

■ LEVEL 1 - INFORMATION

All intelligent decisions are based on adequate information. Before a decision can be made regarding Bible truth, an individual must be convinced of the truth. If there are doubts in the person's mind, he/she will not decide.

The information level is where the facts are presented. To be persuaded in any area of decision, a person must have the facts. The information level provides the various facts upon which an intelligent decision is made. Right decisions cannot be made in any area of life unless an individual has right information.

A very important question to ask is, **"Does the individual have adequate information to make the right decision?"**

In your Bible studies, present clear, convincing evidence from Scripture.

> "**One sentence of Scripture is of more value** than ten thousand of man's ideas or arguments."
>
> *TESTIMONIES,* VOLUME 7, PAGE 71

> "Be very careful how you handle the word, because that word is to make the decisions with the people. **Let the word cut, and not your words.**"
>
> *MANUSCRIPT 42,* 1894

Question 1: What does Jesus say frees us to make right decisions? John 8:32

Answer: ____

Knowing the truth frees a person to make the best possible decision on a given topic. This is why it is so important your Bible study is clear. Knowing the truth leads to the second level: conviction.

■ ■ LEVEL 2 - CONVICTION

Conviction is an inner sense of what God wants. If a person does not follow his convictions, he feels out of balance.

Conviction is an important step in making decisions. Once a person has adequate information, he/she has a sense of what is right and what they ought to do.

> "When persons who are under conviction are not brought to make a decision at the earliest period possible, there is danger that the conviction will gradually wear away."
>
> *EVANGELISM*, PAGE 298

Question 2: When the Roman official, Felix, was under conviction, how did he respond to Paul's appeal? Acts 24:24-25

Answer: ____

Felix stifled his convictions. He hesitated. He delayed. And he never responded to the claims of Christ.

■ ■ ■ LEVEL 3 - DESIRE

Desire is wanting to act. It is necessary to have more than information or even a conviction to do something. A person must also have the desire to act on the information.

The benefits of right-doing or the consequences of wrong-doing will often influence a person's decision. People tend to act in any given situation where the benefits outweigh the liabilities.

Jesus often motivated people by sharing the benefits of making right decisions.

Question 3: How did Jesus respond to Peter's statement, "We have left all and followed you"? Mark 10:29-30

Answer: ____

____

Talk about motivating desire. Jesus said, "Peter, don't worry about what you are giving up, you will receive one hundred times more than you left behind." **People will respond to the gospel when they understand the gospel offers far more than they can imagine.**

■ ■ ■ ■ LEVEL 4 - ACTION

The fourth level or step in getting decisions is action. When a person has adequate information, a conviction of what is right and a desire to do it, action is the next logical step.

J. L. Shuler says,

> "**Decisions** stem out of the interplay of **knowledge, conviction and desire** in a person's mind. When a person's knowledge, and a desire in reference to a given subject reach a certain intensity, the human mind moves into deci-

> sion. The sermons, the Bible studies and the personal talks should be an artful interweaving of the factors of desire and conviction in respect to the given subject."
>
> *PERSUASION*, PAGE 20

As you complete each lesson, invite people to make a decision on the topic you have just studied. During the Bible study, the Holy Spirit is at work convicting their heart of truth and implanting within them a desire to follow it.

Helping people decide to act on the truths they have been studying is often the most difficult part of soul-winning. Many people understand what God wants them to do, but never do it. They believe the truths they have studied, but never act upon them.

Here are three factors that hinder people from making a full decision for Christ.

INHIBITING FACTOR 1 – People tend to hesitate accepting some truths because they don't understand all truth.

RESPONSE – Encourage your Bible students to take "baby steps." Help them act on what they know and God will bring understanding to further truths.

Question 4: What did Jesus say regarding following the light He has revealed on our pathway? John 12:35-36

Answer: ____

As soon as God gives us light, He invites us to walk in it. As we act on the light He has given us, He will give us more light.

INHIBITING FACTOR 2 – People tend to put off changes that make them feel uncomfortable. They tend to procrastinate making decisions that may call for a change in their lives.

RESPONSE – Explain to your Bible students the danger of delay. The longer we wait in making a decision we know we should make, the less likely we are to make it.

Question 5: What challenge did Joshua issue to people struggling with an important decision? Joshua 24:15

Answer: ____

____

The prophets and apostles recognized the urgency of decisions and encouraged people to make definite commitments.

INHIBITING FACTOR 3 – People tend to exaggerate the negative consequences of their decision. The possibility of losing a job, conflict with their loved ones, rejection by their friends, or giving up cherished habits loom large in their minds.

RESPONSE – When we give up what we cherish for the kingdom, God Himself not only meets our needs, He gives us back much, much more.

Question 6: What promise does our Lord give to those who make His kingdom their priority? Matthew 6:31-34

Answer: ____

____

Helping people to accept and decide to do something about the truths they have been studying is often the **most difficult part of soul-winning**. Many individuals are led to study God's word, believe the truths that are presented, but never take any action to bring their lives into conformity with these teachings.

The Bible instructor should seek to lead his student gently, firmly and prayerfully to a decision. **Never give up until the battle is won and the student is safely on the side of Christ.**

Ellen White shares this important principle in a letter she wrote in 1890.

> "Many are convicted of sin, and feel their need of a sin-pardoning Savior; but they are merely dissatisfied with their pursuits and aims, and if there is not a decided application of the truth to their hearts, if words are not spoken at the right moment, calling for decision from the weight of evidence already presented, the convicted ones pass on without identifying themselves with Christ, the golden opportunity passes, and they have not yielded, and they go farther and farther away from the truth, farther away from Jesus and never take their stand on the Lord's side. Christ's claims upon them are to be made plain. The people should be urged to decide just now to be on the Lord's side.
>
> *LETTER 29,* 1890

When personal labor is done in the homes of people, and you ask the people for a decision, there will be positive results. The following statement from Ellen White is a wonderful promise and was made in reference to Bible work or personal work.

"Accompanied by the power of persuasion, the power of prayer, the power of the love of God, this work will not, cannot, be without fruit."
EVANGELISM, PAGE 459

FOUR DIFFERENT BASIC APPEALS

1. The greatness of God's love – John 3:16
Picture the love of God and the death of Christ for the individual.

2. The influence of their example – Romans 14:7
Stress the influence of a decision on loved ones and friends.

3. The power of choice – Matthew 7:13-14
Show your Bible study contacts the choice God has given them between life and death. Impress the thought that there will be only two classes at the end of the world, the saved and the unsaved.

4. The danger of delay – Matthew 25:10; II Corinthians 6:2
Show the danger of delay and the closing of an opportunity to be saved.

Prayer is a powerful means of calling for decision. **Pray for the person to have courage to make a decision for Christ. Ask them to pray if it is appropriate to do so.**

> "Pray with these souls, by faith bringing them to the foot of the cross. Carry their minds with your mind, and fix the eye of faith where you look upon Jesus, the sin-bearer. Get them to look away from their poor, sinful selves to the Savior, and the victory is won."
> *TESTIMONIES*, VOLUME 6, PAGE 67

If an individual is struggling with a decision on any given topic, ask them if they would like you to pray with them about their concerns.

Ask if there is something specific that is holding them back which they would like you to present to the Lord in prayer. Encourage them to personally pray about their problem.

Regularly, when people pray about something, God convicts them to act. Solid, spiritual decisions are made in the context of prayer.

You can be an effective soul-winner. You can see results for the kingdom of God. God will do more through your faithful witness than you could possibly imagine. **Invite people to make decisions and watch what God does**.

EXPECT DECISIONS!

CHAPTER 12

REAPING A HARVEST

There are times when a farmer reaps a bumper crop. A bumper crop is an unusually large harvest and may come only once in a farmer's lifetime. For example, an apple farmer may have such an outstanding harvest that where his trees normally produced five tons of apples, they now produce fifteen. Bumper crops are something special. They are exceptional harvests.

God is preparing for a bumper crop at the end of time. His unusually large final harvest will surprise us. Think of it. Jesus invites us to participate with Him in reaping the largest harvest of souls in the history of the world.

Question 1: In the first century, the disciples were looking forward to a future harvest. What did Jesus say to them about the harvest? John 4:35

Answer: ____

____

The harvest was **ready**. It was right before their eyes and they did not see it. The Samaritans were open to receiving the gospel. Once again, in our day, the harvest is ripe.

Question 2: What prediction does the prophet Joel give about an end-time harvest? Joel 3:13-14

Answer: ____

____

God is preparing a final end-time harvest of honest-hearted people all over the world. Tens of thousands of pastors and lay people are cooperating with God in His final work.

Now is the time to lift our vision to what Christ is doing in the world. This is the time for a renewed sense that God is reaping His final harvest right now. God says we can have the Holy Spirit right now if we only seek, ask and believe.

> "The descent of the Holy Spirit upon the church is looked forward to as in the future; but it is the privilege of the church to have it now. Seek for it, pray for it, believe for it. We must have it, and heaven is waiting to bestow it."
>
> *EVANGELISM*, PAGE 701

As we witness to people in our sphere of influence, whether it is in the home, on the job, at school or during our daily activities, God will bless our efforts. As we plan to reach our neighborhoods, small towns, villages and major metropolitan areas, God will bless our work.

As we sow seeds, God will give us a harvest. He will especially bless every Bible study we give. We have this promise from a letter written by Ellen White in 1901.

> "**All who can, should do personal labor.** As they go from house to house, explaining the Scriptures to the people in a clear, simple manner, God makes the truth powerful to save. **The Savior blesses those who do this work.**"
>
> *LETTER 108*, 1901

HOW DO WE REAP A HARVEST FROM OUR BIBLE STUDY WORK?

1. DECISIONS IN THE HOME

• *Through Bible studies*

Some people will make decisions in their home, begin attending church, eventually accept baptism and become a part of God's remnant church. Others may not make a decision in the home setting, but will make a decision if they are in a public evangelistic environment.

• *Through home video or DVD evangelism*

Some people will not make a final decision during the Bible study, but will do so when they go through the message again in home evangelism.

2. DECISIONS IN PUBLIC EVANGELISTIC MEETINGS

Another effective way to get decisions is for your Bible study interests to attend public evangelistic meetings.

• ***Live evangelist***

The public evangelistic meetings can be conducted either by a full-time evangelist, pastor evangelist or lay evangelist. (The graphics from *New Beginnings* or *Revelation of Hope* can be used.)

You can take a handbill about the meetings with you as you visit your Bible study students. You might say something like this:

"We're so happy for the relationship we've developed with you over the past few weeks/ months. We're thankful for the opportunity of studying the Bible together. A good friend of mine by the name of __________ is going to have a multimedia series of meetings here in town soon. He will be using computer graphics and talking about topics like the times we are living in today, the crisis the world is in and how to really know God. His meetings will feature the prophetic themes of Daniel and Revelation. I'd love to have you as my guest at these meetings. Do you think you might be able to come this weekend?"

Give them the brochure and tell them a little about the first meeting or two. **Sign them up** on the pre-registration form. (Pre-registration sample in the appendix on Page 153)

Do not end your Bible studies with them at this point. If they come the opening weekend they will learn about the entire series. By this time they may be so excited that they will want to keep coming. If they come only to the opening weekend, continue your studies with them. If they continue coming, suggest they bring their lessons to the meetings and review them there.

If you can **get your Bible study contacts to come to the meetings**, they will make giant steps forward. There is something about the dynamics of public meetings that helps people make significant decisions.

• *Video and DVD "Play-It" Campaigns*

The public evangelistic meetings can be conducted by using the *Discoveries in Prophecy* or *Revelation of Hope* video series. The *New Beginnings* evangelistic DVD "Play-It" version with scripts and graphics may also be used.

One of the proven successful ways to reap baptismal results is through the video campaigns. Tens of thousands around the world have come to the Lord and the "Three Angels' Message" of Revelation through video campaigns conducted by pastors and lay members.

Many have used the *Discoveries in Prophecy* and *Revelation of Hope* videos, which have been translated into 47 languages. Preparation for a video series is the same as that done for a live evangelist. The only difference is that the videos take the place of a live presentation.

New Beginnings is a full set of evangelistic sermons prepared on DVD by *It Is Written Television,* and sponsored by ASI—Adventist-Laymen's Services and Industries. The "Play-It" version can be used just like the video series, as it contains fully-illustrated, recorded presentations with dynamic graphics.

Listed below are helpful tips for conducting a successful reaping series of meetings by video or DVD. (See *Change Your World for God* evangelistic planning manual or *New Beginnings Training Manual* for full details.)

GETTING STARTED

1. Decide what series you will use

❏ *Discoveries in Prophecy*
❏ *Revelation of Hope*
❏ *New Beginnings*

2. Decide where to conduct your meetings

❏ Home
❏ Church
❏ Public Auditorium

3. Decide on the number of nights per week

The length of the campaign will be determined by the series you choose and the number of nights (per week) you will hold meetings.

❏ *Discoveries in Prophecy* – 24 sessions
❏ *Revelation of Hope* – 27 sessions
❏ *New Beginnings* – 26 sessions

4. Choose the committee for the campaign

A core group of four-to-six people is needed for a home meeting. More people are needed for an evangelistic meeting in a church or public auditorium.

Once you have established your core group of workers, we recommend you have a fellowship dinner meeting at your home. This meeting will assist staff members in organizing and will allow you to answer any basic questions regarding the evangelistic meetings.

5. Pre-register every Bible study contact

Pre-register every Bible Study contact with a program reservation form. (See Page 153)

Send invitations to:

- ❑ Every Bible study contact
- ❑ Friends
- ❑ Relatives
- ❑ Interests from all media ministries
- ❑ People from the interest list

6. Conduct the reaping evangelistic meetings

Materials needed

- ❑ Videotapes, DVD or computer graphics
- ❑ Lessons or outlines that correspond with tapes
- ❑ Bibles
- ❑ Decision cards

Note: The full-time evangelist will have his own instructions for the meetings.

The pastor or lay member conducting the meetings through the videos or DVDs can get specific instructions for conducting an evangelistic meeting through the *Change Your World For God* evangelistic planning manual by Mark and Ernestine Finley or *New Beginnings DV D Evangelism Training Manual*.

The meetings are about to begin

Your home or small room in the church now becomes an evangelistic center.

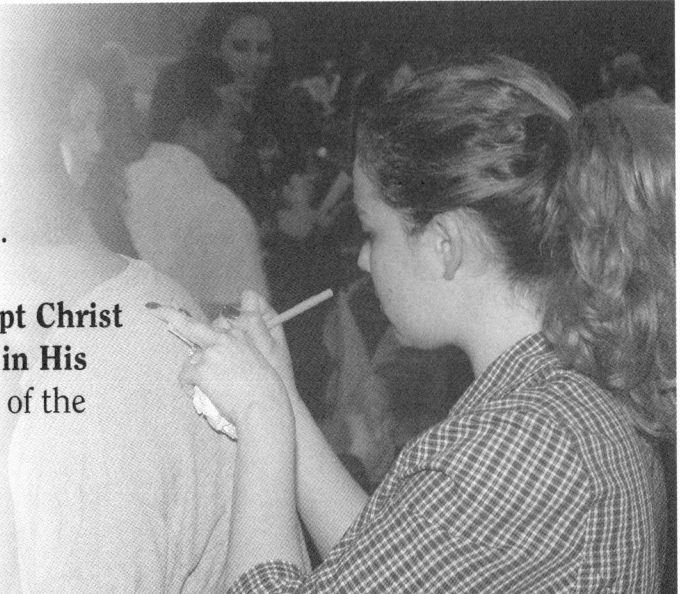

7. Reap a harvest

God will pour out His Holy Spirit through you. You will reap a harvest.

In your home, church or hall, **people will accept Christ and His truth for these last days and will be saved in His kingdom**. There will be people in heaven as a result of the reaping meetings you have conducted.

You can have the absolute certainty of success. The seed of the word of God will be planted in the soil of hundreds and thousands of minds. These seeds will spring up to an eternal harvest of souls for Christ. The seed has life-giving, life-changing power. Plant it in the soil of minds and hearts and there will be an abundant harvest of souls through your ministry. In eternity we can look back and measure the results.

Question 3: What vision of God's work on earth did God give the Apostle John in Revelation? Revelation 18:1

Answer: ____

____

In one of the **most magnificent visions in the Bible**, John saw the earth lightened with the glory of God. Ellen White describes exactly how this prophecy will be fulfilled.

> "I saw jets of light shining from cities and villages, and from the high places and the low places of the earth. God's word was obeyed, and as a result there were memorials for Him in every city and village. His truth was proclaimed throughout the world. **Hundreds and thousands were seen visiting families, and opening before them the word of God.** Hearts were convicted by the power of the Holy Spirit, and a spirit of genuine conversion was manifest. On every side doors were thrown open to the proclamation of the truth. The world seemed to be lightened with the heavenly influence."
>
> *EVANGELISM*, PAGE 699

You can be part of the fulfillment of this prophecy—you can be one of God's streams of light. **Every Bible instructor is a point of light.**

You will be forever thankful that you got involved in the most thrilling and lasting work in the world—soul-winning. **There is power in the word of God.** Study it! Share it with others! It will bring everlasting, eternal results.

We as church members have an **awesome responsibility**. This responsibility can be combined with an **awesome promise**, summed up on the last page of the book *Evangelism*.

> "Our watchword is to be, Onward, ever onward! Angels of heaven will go before us to prepare the way. **Our burden for the regions beyond can never be laid down till the whole earth is lightened with the glory of the Lord."**
>
> *EVANGELISM*, PAGE 707

God's promises are sure! There will be a great harvest! Praise God!

CHAPTER 13

SUCCESS IN BIBLE WORK

What farmer would plant crops and not expect a harvest? Whether you are a full-time farmer with hundreds of acres of corn or a backyard gardener with a few tomato plants, you anticipate the harvest. You look forward to the day you can pick your produce. The purpose of planting is not just growing the crops, it's reaping a harvest.

Just as farmers anxiously await a harvest, **soul-winners long for a harvest**. They long to see the people they are praying for and studying the Bible with won for the kingdom of God. They embrace God's promise, "In due season we shall reap if we do not lose heart." (Galatians 6:9)

God promises to bless our faithfulness. He will bring the seeds we have sown to harvest. His promise is sure. You can be a successful soul-winner. Jesus illustrates the secrets of successful soul-winning in His own life. You too can experience success. There are three simple principles to successful Bible work. They are the **ABC's of success**.

ABC

A – ASK

Ask God to give you spirit-anointed eyes to see people as winnable.

Question 1: What did Jesus say regarding the Canaanite woman? Matthew 15:28

Answer:____

Question 2: What amazing statement did Jesus make to one of the scribes? Mark 12:34

Answer:____

In each instance **Jesus saw people as winnable**. He complimented them because He was genuinely interested in them. His confidence in them opened their hearts to the gospel. They became what He saw them as. **Jesus had vision.**

Vision is the ability to see with the eyes of God. Most people have sight, but only a few people have vision. Most people have eyes, only a few people really see.

Vision is the ability to see beyond what is to what can be. Vision penetrates through the present. It sees the possibilities. Vision looks beyond the problems to the potential.

Jesus saw everyone He came in contact with as winnable. He saw people not as they were, but as refined and ennobled by His grace. He saw the following people not for who they were, but who they could become.

Peter • Not as an ignorant, loud-mouthed, cursing, smelly fisherman, but as a powerful preacher.

Matthew • Not as a conniving, shrewd, lying, dishonest tax collector, but as a careful, meticulous chronicler of the gospels.

Mary Magdalene • Not as an immoral, lewd, low-class woman of ill repute, but as a tenderhearted, loving witness of His love.

The Roman Centurion • Not as a rough, hardened leader of the opposition, but as a candidate for the kingdom of God.

Nicodemus • Not as a legalistic, argumentative, opinionated Pharisee, but as a sincere seeker after truth.

Jesus saw people as **valuable**. He saw people as **winnable**. He saw people as redeemed for the kingdom of God. Since he saw them that way, they rose to meet His expectations. They became what He believed them to be.

B – BELIEVE

Believe it is God's will for you to have success.

It is the will of God that our churches grow. It is the will of God for the lost to be found. "There is more joy in heaven over one soul who repents." (Luke 15:7)

Question 1: Why were the disciples unable to cast the demons out of a little child? Matthew 17:20 (first phrase)

Answer: ____

Question 2: What did Jesus say was the necessary ingredient to see mountains of difficulties removed? Matthew 17:20

Answer: ____

Belief or faith is the hand that reaches up and grasps God's power. Faith is powerful because it unites us with an all-powerful God. Faith moves mountains because it puts us in touch with a God who moves mountains.

PRAYER AND FAITH ARE THE TWINS OF SUCCESS

Pray, "Lord, please give me a burden for lost human beings all around me. Lord, give me a desire to see men and women reconciled to You."

God will not allow your work to go without reward.

> "God will not permit this precious work for Him to go unrewarded. He will crown with success every humble effort made in His name."
>
> *GOSPEL WORKERS*, PAGE 192

Believe God's grace is stronger than any obstacle holding the person you are studying with back from making a decision for Christ. Believe God's power is stronger than the chains that bind people in sin. Believe God's truth is stronger than deception and error. Believe, and you will be able to move mountains.

C – COME CLOSE

Come close to people as Jesus did.

Jesus cared for people. He cared about their heartaches. He always got close enough to people to know what their needs were.

Question 3: What short question reveals one of Jesus' most powerful soul-winning success secrets? John 1:38

Answer:____

Jesus was always interested in the people around him. He was asking "**What are you seeking?** What are your longings? What needs do you have? I am interested in meeting them."

Throughout the following chapters of John's gospel, Jesus demonstrated His immense care for people by meeting a variety of their needs.

❦ **John 2: Jesus met a social need.** At the wedding feast at Cana, the host ran out of wine. Jesus turned six stone jars of water into refreshing new wine. He alleviated the host's social embarrassment.

❦ **John 3: Jesus met a spiritual need.** Nicodemus, a Pharisee, asked for a meeting in the dead of night. Jesus showed him exactly what he was looking for and how to get it. He said, "You must be born again." He satisfied Nicodemus' soul, which was longing for salvation.

❦ **John 4: Jesus met an emotional need** with the woman at the well. This woman had gone through six husbands. Jesus offered her emotional support, treating her with kindness.

❦ **John 5: Jesus met a physical need.** This man had lain by the pool of Bethseda for 38 years. Jesus said, "Do you want to be made whole?" then healed him.

❦ **John 6: Jesus met another physical need**—that of physical nourishment. Jesus was confronted with thousands of hungry people on a hillside. Jesus received five barley loaves and two fish from a young lad and multiplied them. Thousands ate and were filled.

Jesus is the One who can meet every human need. He reached people where they were, touched them at their point of need and gave them a glimpse of His wonderful love.

Follow Jesus' example to achieve success!

> "**Christ's method alone will give true success** in reaching the people. The Savior mingled with men as one who desired their good. He showed His sympathy for them, ministered to their needs, and won their confidence. Then He bade them, 'Follow Me.'"
>
> *MINISTRY OF HEALING*, PAGE 143

Jesus first ministered to people's needs, then he asked them to follow Him. If you want to be successful, get involved in the lives of your Bible study contacts.

> "Your **success** will not depend so much upon your knowledge and accomplishments, as upon your ability to find your way to the heart. By **being social and coming close to the people**, you may turn the current of their thoughts more readily than by the most able discourses."
>
> *GOSPEL WORKERS*, PAGE 193

Let's review

What are the ABC's of success in Bible study work?

A ______________________________

B ______________________________

C ______________________________

As the result of Jesus' loving ministry, tens of thousands were baptized when the Holy Spirit was poured out on the day of Pentecost. The seeds of love and truth sown by Jesus in people's hearts sprouted and grew to a glorious harvest.

Again in our day, the spirit will produce a great harvest. The earth will be lightened with His glory. The latter-rain power of the Holy Spirit will be poured out. Thousands will be converted in a day. Every honest-hearted person on the face of planet earth will have one final opportunity to accept or reject God's offer of salvation. **All the seeds sown for millenniums will spring up for one final harvest**.

Think of it: **God has chosen us to prepare a dying world for His soon return**. He has chosen us to share His love with the people around us. He has chosen us to sow the seeds and participate with Him in earth's final harvest. What a privilege! What an honor! And to top it off, He guarantees us success.

Think of what it will be like to have a mother come up to you in heaven with tears streaming down her face saying, "Thank you for giving Bible studies to my son. He is here because God used you."

Think of someone throwing their arms around you and delightfully saying, "Our home was different because of you. I remember those Bible studies every Friday night. You led Mom and Dad to Christ. We are here as a family because of you."

Or a woman says, "Thank you for what you did for my husband. He was a drinking, cursing, angry man until Jesus changed him during your Bible studies."

The stories go on and on and on through all eternity. Stories of an answered prayer offered for someone's son or daughter. Stories of miraculous conversions through a piece of literature distributed, stories of lives changed through an invitation to an evangelistic meeting.

Soul-winning is the most wonderful work in the world.
Only in eternity will we learn of our true success
and receive our final reward.

CHAPTER 14

NURTURE AND FOLLOW-UP

Evangelism is incomplete without a **comprehensive strategy to nurture new converts**. Jesus' great commission is not merely to baptize. It is to make disciples. "Disciple-making" is not the result of impromptu decisions in evangelistic meetings. It is a **process** resulting from systematic nurture of new converts.

Baptism is not a magic formula to solve all spiritual problems. It is not a panacea to deliver people from all their difficulties. **Baptism is not the end of a spiritual journey, but the beginning** of a new life of fellowship with Christ in the context of His church.

Often, immediately after baptism, new believers are faced with some of their most serious challenges. The devil zeroes in on them. His goal is to sever their relationship with the body of Christ. New believers need to be nurtured in order to grow and become mature Christians.

> "**After individuals have been converted** to the truth, **they need to be looked after**. The zeal of many ministers seems to fail as soon as a measure of success attends their efforts. They do not realize that these newly converted ones need nursing,—watchful attention, help and encouragement. **These should not be left alone**, a prey to Satan's most powerful temptations; they need to be **educated in regard to their duties**, to be **kindly dealt** with to be led along, and to be **visited and prayed with**. These souls need the meat apportioned to every man in due season."
>
> *EVANGELISM*, PAGE 351

Question 1: According to the book of Acts, how long did Paul labor in the same city? Acts 18:11

Answer:____

The Apostle Paul was so concerned about nurturing his new converts that he spent **a year-and-a-half** teaching them the principles of God's word in Corinth.

After individuals have been instructed through Bible studies or evangelistic meetings and are baptized, it is vital for them to continue studying God's word. It is also important to educate them in the Seventh-day Adventist Christian lifestyle. It is very likely that some new converts will become discouraged shortly after their baptism.

Apostasies will not be needlessly high if there is:

• A carefully-planned process of **after-care** to reinforce their new doctrinal understanding.
• A program set in place to **teach the new believers how to keep growing spiritually**. An understanding of how to have a meaningful devotional life, as well as uplifting family worship, is vital to spiritual growth.
• A measure of **tolerance for their mistakes** as they are given latitude to grow.
• An **organized visitation program** set in motion immediately after their baptism.
• A conscious effort to **integrate them into the social network** of the church.
• A process to **teach them how to live** the Seventh-day Adventist Christian **lifestyle**.
• An attempt to involve them in some kind of witnessing or **outreach program**. New believers become strong if they are actively involved in sharing their newfound faith.

Question 2: What happened to newly-baptized believers in the book of Acts? Acts 2:41-42

Answer: ____

After new believers were baptized, they continued steadfastly in the apostles' doctrine. They were not baptized and left alone. They continued strong in the faith.

Question 3: How did these new believers continue in the apostles' doctrine? Acts 2:42, 46-47

Answer: ____

The book of **Acts gives us insight into solid nurture** and follow-up work. The Scripture tells how the disciples met the physical, mental, emotional, social and spiritual needs of the large number of new converts to the Christian faith.

Elements of New Testament Nurture

Personal Devotional Life — In the New Testament there is evidence of a vibrant devotional life and a personal life of prayer. (Acts 4:13, 31)

Fellowship House-to-House — In the New Testament, spiritual and social needs were met in small groups as they broke bread or shared a common meal and prayed together. (Acts 2:42)

Corporate Worship and Praise — In the New Testament, spiritual and social needs were also met through Sabbath worship, biblical preaching and praise. (Acts 2:46)

Involvement and Witness — In the New Testament, new believers grew spiritually as they were actively involved in witness and faith-sharing. The early Christians were specifically involved in ministering to physical needs in their community as well as sharing the gospel.

- The word of God spread. (Acts 6:7, 8:4)
- Believers sold their possessions—no one lacked. (Acts 4:32-35)

Baptism is the symbol of a new birth. It is not an indication that the new convert is fully mature. It is the **responsibility of the church** to take careful steps to help each church member develop a deep, abiding relationship with Christ and a secure relationship with His church.

Question 4: What concern did Luke express regarding Theophilus' own faith? Luke 1:4

Answer:____

It is one thing to be informed of truth. It is another thing to be certain of what you believe. Luke longed for Theophilus to be anchored in the certainty of truth.

Question 5: Of what does Paul advise new believers to be aware? Colossians 2:8; Galatians 3:1

Answer:____

Paul warned new believers to beware of anyone who would take them away from the truth that they were taught. The way to do that is to continue studying God's word.

Question 6: What counsel did Jesus give Peter regarding new believers? John 21:15-17

Answer:____

"This was a work in which Peter had but little experience; but he could not be complete in Christian life unless he learned to feed the lambs, those who are young in the faith."

EVANGELISM, PAGE 346

STEPS FOR ESTABLISHING AND RETAINING NEW CONVERTS

The ten steps for establishing and nurturing new converts will be discussed in the context of the four specific elements of New Testament nurture:

- ❑ **Personal devotions**
- ❑ **Home fellowship**
- ❑ **Corporate worship**
- ❑ **Active involvement**

❑ Personal Devotional Life

STEP 1: EDUCATE NEW CONVERTS ON HOW TO GROW SPIRITUALLY

Part of the nurturing process is helping each new believer develop his/her own devotional life. The goal is to assist them in having a vibrant spiritual life through personal and family worship. This type of teaching can be modeled as we pray with new converts and involve them in prayer groups.

PRACTICAL IDEAS

❦ Give them the yearly **devotional book**; set a time to read the first few chapters with them to help them get started.

❦ **Share how** to have a meaningful devotional life. As you visit new believers in their homes, share how to start their own personal devotions using the yearly devotional book. Share your own testimony of how blessed you are daily by doing this.

❦ Teach them to pray with the **ACTS model**. Pray with them. Share with them how to include the following aspects of prayer.

A **Adoration and Praise**
C **Confession and Repentance**
T **Thanksgiving and Gratitude**
S **Supplication**

> "It is not in God's purpose that the church shall be sustained by life drawn from the minister. They are to have root in themselves... Everyone who claims to be a Christian is to bear the responsibility of keeping himself in harmony with the guidance of the word of God. God holds **each soul accountable for following, for himself, the pattern given in the life of Christ** and for having a character that is cleansed and sanctified."
>
> *EVANGELISM*, PAGE 343

> "The interest awakened should be followed up by personal labor—visiting, holding Bible readings, teaching how to search the Scriptures, pray with families and interested ones, seeking to deepen the impression made upon hearts and consciences."
>
> *EVANGELISM*, PAGE 343

STEP 2: REPEAT THE BIBLICAL MESSAGE A SECOND TIME

One of the ways in which new converts can be strengthened is to review the essentials of Scripture a second time. This reinforces truth in their minds. Merely hearing truth once is not enough. Restudying it solidifies a new convert's convictions.

Invite them to a small group Bible study in your home

Do not assume that just because a new convert has completed a Bible course or attended evangelistic meetings, they fully understand the message. Repeating it a second time solidifies it in the mind of a new believer. It anchors their faith. Since new believers are often eager to share their newfound faith, a repetition of the great truths of the Bible also provides them with an excellent opportunity to invite their friends.

Ellen White reaffirms the principle of repetition in these words:

> "After the first efforts have been made in a place by giving a course of lectures, there is really **greater necessity for a second course** than for the first. The truth is new and startling, and the people need to have the same truth presented the second time, to get the points distinct and the ideas fixed in the mind."
>
> *EVANGELISM*, PAGE 334

PRACTICAL IDEA

❦ To "fasten the truth" upon the mind, we recommend lessons such as, *Unsealing Daniel's Mysteries, Revelation Speaks* or *Life in the Son.*

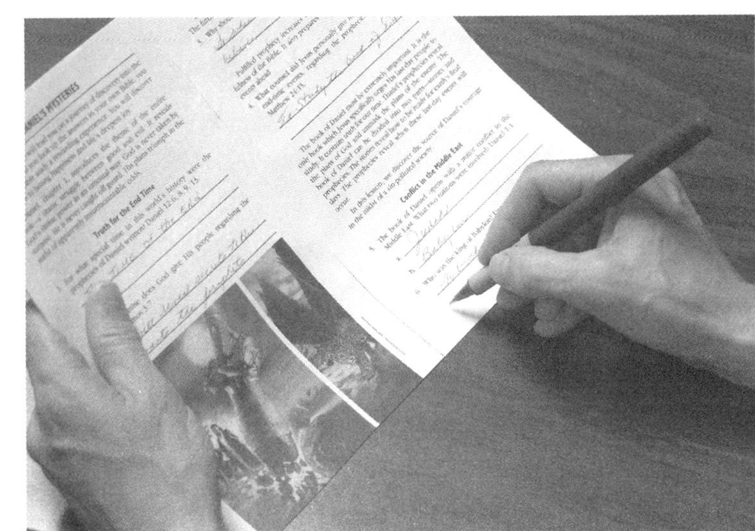

Unsealing Daniel's Mysteries is a series of studies on the book of Daniel, chapter-by-chapter. It focuses on the practical lifestyle/character issues in Daniel. These studies deepen faith, encourage faithfulness and enhance a rich devotional life. There are 12 lessons in the series, especially designed for use in small groups.

Revelation Speaks is a chapter-by-chapter series of studies on the book of Revelation. The lessons can be used in a group or as individual study. However, we recommend that new converts come together once a week at the church or in a home and review the lessons together.

Life in the Son is a series on the book of John. As a rich devotional study on the life of Christ, it is a change from the doctrinal emphasis on prophecy. This series emphasizes lessons from the life of Christ.

> "The new converts will need to be instructed by faithful teachers of God's word, that they may increase in a knowledge and love of the truth, and may grow to the full stature of men and women in Christ Jesus."
>
> *EVANGELISM*, PAGE 337

Important—Small groups and follow-up classes at the church for new believers contribute to a growing Christian life, but they do not replace a personal devotional life.

STEP 3: EDUCATE NEW BELIEVERS ON HOW TO HAVE A BETTER LIFESTYLE

Since discipleship applies to the totality of life, continuing instruction in the health aspects of God's last-day message is critically important.

Question 7: What counsel did the apostle Paul give the new churches in Rome? Romans 12:1; I Corinthians 6:19-20

Answer:____

Paul's counsel to the new believers in Rome was directed at the importance of **surrendering both the mind and body** to Christ. This apostle, who so eloquently preached that salvation was through faith, was also concerned about the physical health of the new believers.

> "Ministers frequently neglect these important branches of the work—**health reform, spiritual gifts, systematic benevolenc**e and the great branches of the **missionary work.**"
>
> *EVANGELISM*, PAGE 343

Many new believers have been instructed through Bible studies and evangelistic meetings on the harmful effects of tobacco, alcohol and unclean meat. Many would like to follow principles of **health reform**; however, they may not know how to change their lifestyle. They have learned about tithing and **systematic benevolence**, but may not know how to incorporate it into their budget. They have a desire to get involved in some kind of **missionary work**, sharing their newfound faith with others, but don't know where to begin. This provides a great opportunity for pastors and established church members to nurture new believers.

PRACTICAL IDEAS

❦ **Healthful Cooking** - Conduct a Natural Lifestyle Cooking School (*Natural Lifestyle Cooking* by Mark and Ernestine Finley is an entire series of cooking and nutrition classes.)

They cover areas such as:

- Homemade Breadmaking Made Easy
- Making Breakfast a Better Meal
- How to Have a Balanced Menu
- Getting Adequate Protein Without Using Meat
- Simple Healthful Desserts

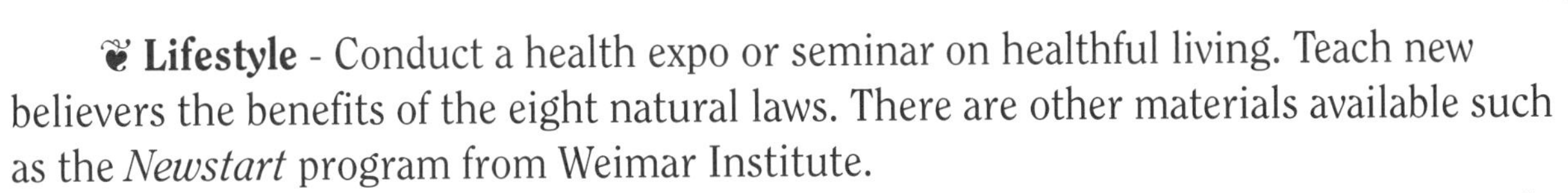

❦ **Lifestyle** - Conduct a health expo or seminar on healthful living. Teach new believers the benefits of the eight natural laws. There are other materials available such as the *Newstart* program from Weimar Institute.

❦ **Systematic Benevolence** - Conduct a program on stewardship. We recommend G. Edward Reid's seminar and book titled, *It's Your Money! Isn't It?*

❦ **Spiritual Gifts** - Conduct a seminar on spiritual gifts. Study materials are a available to help people discover their special talents and gifts.

❦ **Missionary work** - Conduct *Lighting Your World For God* training classes. Get them involved in a Bible study ministry program *(Soup & Salvation).*

❑ Home Fellowship

STEP 4: IMPLEMENT A VISITATION PROGRAM

Convincing evidence demonstrates that many new converts are lost because they are not visited. We should not just "dip them" and "drop them."

Visitation is extremely critical if new members are to grow in Christ and feel at home in the church. It is possible for a new convert to be **doctrinally convinced, but not socially integrated** into the church. Although they have been baptized, they still feel like an outsider. They feel uncomfortable with this new group of people. The following are some things we can do to help them feel at home.

PRACTICAL IDEAS

❦ Organize visitation teams to visit the new converts. Church growth studies indicate the more friends a person has in the church, the less likely he/she will drop out.

> "The work should not be left prematurely. See that all are intelligent in the truth, established in the faith, and interested in every branch of the work, before leaving them for another field. And then, **like the apostle Paul, visit them often** to see how they do."
>
> *Evangelism*, Page 338

❦ **Love and care** for these new believers can be practically demonstrated in a brief visit. If we can **get new converts reading** the Bible, in harmony with the writings of Ellen White, they will grow into strong Christians.

> "*Patriarchs and Prophets* and *Great Controversy* are books that are especially adapted to those who have newly come to the faith, that they may be established in the truth...in *Desire of Ages, Patriarchs and Prophets, Great Controversy* and *Daniel and the Revelation*, there is precious instruction. **These books must be regarded as of special importance, and every effort should be made to get them before the people.**"
>
> *LETTER 229*, 1903

The visitation schedule can be organized as follows:

- MONTH 1 – Visit and give a copy of *Patriarchs and Prophets*
- MONTH 2 – Visit and give a copy of *The Great Controversy*
- MONTH 3 – Visit and give a copy of *Desire of Ages*
- MONTH 4 – Visit and give the yearly devotional book
- MONTH 5 – Visit and give a copy of the *Adventist Review*
- MONTH 6 – Visit and give a copy of *Studying Together*

We suggest visitation teams be organized so that different church officers and members deliver the books each month. This broadens the base. Later we will discuss a particular plan for spiritual guardians.

❦ **Send a note indicating they are in your thoughts**. In between the monthly visits, the pastor/church members can send a note to the new believers demonstrating their care for them.

❦ **Give them a casual, friendly phone call**. Making a short casual phone call inbetween visits will help to solidify new believers in the church.

If they miss church, you can send them a copy of the bulletin and a tape of the sermon. If they continue to miss church, be sure to give them a call to determine if there is any serious problem. The longer you wait, the more difficult it will be to get them back.

STEP 5: IMPLEMENT A SPIRITUAL GUARDIANSHIP PLAN

This plan assigns each new member a **spiritual guardian**. The goal is to find church members with like interests and of a similar background. The established church member becomes a spiritual guardian for the new member. Once the new member is rooted in the church, he/she can become a spiritual guardian for the next new member.

> "**In Christ we are all members of one family**. God is our Father, and He expects us to take an interest in the members of His household, not a casual interest, but a decided, continual interest."
>
> *EVANGELISM*, PAGE 352

HOW TO BE A SPIRITUAL GUARDIAN

Your major role is to be a friend. Your role is not to be a spiritual policeman.
You certainly are not a judge of what they do wrong.
You are a **mentor** for the new convert. He/she is the mentee.
New believers need someone to look to—to help them grow spiritually
as well as physically, emotionally, mentally and socially.
Show your care as you seek to come close to them.

PRACTICAL IDEAS

❦ PRAY – Pray for them regularly.
❦ VISIT – Visit them once a month. Use the visitation program mentioned earlier using the gift books.
❦ CALL – Call them inbetween the monthly visit.
❦ SEND – Send a note on special occasions such as birthdays, Thanksgiving, Christmas etc. It is also good to send a casual note with a few words of encouragement.
❦ INVITE – Invite them to dinner once every other month. The opposite month have them participate with you in preparing dinner for other people. This will help them learn how to become a spiritual guardian.
❦ DO – Do something together once a month to build a deeper friendship.
❦ JOIN – Join *Soup & Salvation* with them.
❦ WITNESS – Get them involved in going out and sharing their faith.

STEP 6: DEAL TENDERLY, KINDLY AND PATIENTLY WITH NEW BELIEVERS

Many new converts have made great sacrifices to become part of God's remnant church. They have changed their lifestyle. As a result of accepting Bible truth, some have faced opposition from their friends and relatives. Now is the time to deal kindly, tenderly and patiently with them. **Most apostasies** take place because new **believers have been hurt, offended, or had a conflict** with the pastor or some other church member. As we lovingly reach out, many will be solid in the church. Ellen White says,

> "**Those who have newly come to the faith should be patiently and tenderly dealt with**, and it is the duty of the older members of the church to devise ways and means to provide help and sympathy and instruction for those who have conscientiously withdrawn from other churches for the truth's sake, and thus cut themselves off from the pastoral labor to which they have been accustomed. The church has a special responsibility laid upon her to attend to these souls who have followed the first rays of light they have received; and if the members of the church neglect this duty, they will be unfaithful to the trust that God has given them."
>
> *EVANGELISM*, PAGE 351

STEP 7: INTEGRATE NEW BELIEVERS INTO THE SOCIAL ASPECT OF THE CHURCH

Inviting these new members **home to dinner** is a wonderful way to get acquainted with them better on a social basis. This will help them to feel loved and accepted.

Plan **church social** events such as picnics, camping trips, vespers at the beach etc., that these new believers can become involved in.

❑ Corporate Worship and Praise

STEP 8: COME INTO GOD'S HOUSE EVERY SABBATH AND WORSHIP HIM

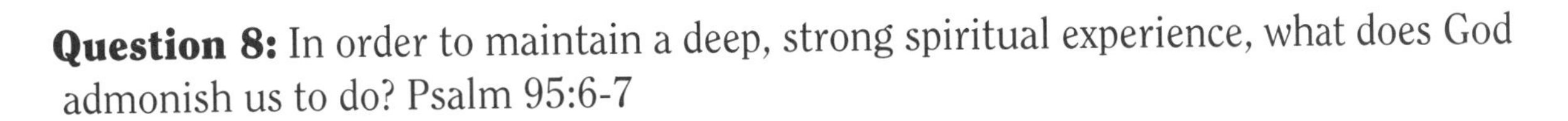

Question 8: In order to maintain a deep, strong spiritual experience, what does God admonish us to do? Psalm 95:6-7

Answer:____

New believers will grow in their spiritual experience as they come to God's house each Sabbath. We receive strength from one another.

Question 9: What are believers counseled to do each week? Hebrews 10:25

Answer: ____

Church members are not to forsake the assembling of themselves together. They are to come once a week into the temple of God and worship Him.

Question 10: What will the redeemed be doing every Sabbath in the new earth? Isaiah 66:23

Answer: ____

Yes, what a wonderful experience the redeemed will have from Sabbath to Sabbath as they come to worship God!

REASONS FOR AND VALUE OF CORPORATE WORSHIP

To praise and give thanks – Ephesians 5:19-20; Psalm 150; Psalm 67:3
To hear the word of God – Acts 13:44
To sing – Hebrews: 2:12
To pray – Acts 16:13
To report all God has done – Acts 14:27
To encourage one another to good works – Hebrews 10:24-25
To study – II Timothy 2:15

"Our people should not be made to think that they need to listen to a sermon every Sabbath. Many who listen frequently to sermons, even though the truth be presented in clear lines, learn but little. Often it would be **more profitable if the Sabbath meetings were of the nature of a Bible class study**."

EVANGELISM, PAGE 348

❑ Involvement and Witness

STEP 9: EDUCATE NEW BELIEVERS IN SOUL-WINNING

When new believers share their faith, the faith they share strengthens. We are blessed as we give. Ellen White states it well when she says,

"Strength to resist evil is best gained by aggressive service."

ACTS OF APOSTLES, PAGE 105

Benefits of being involved in soul-winning

There are at least two decided benefits to be gained in getting new believers involved in soul-winning.

First, soul-winning work drives an individual to his/her knees. It also makes one dependent upon Scripture. It will dramatically strengthen the individual's faith. The questions others ask will lead them to study the word.

Secondly, new converts have a network of friends who can be won. They have family members who will be eager to know what they believe.

Question 11: What did the new believers do in the book of Acts after their baptism? Acts 8:4

Answer:____

These new converts were **involved** in active soul-winning. They went everywhere preaching the word. Once you come to Christ you want to tell others about salvation and His word.

> "Unite with the Spirit of the living God to present a bulwark around our people and around our youth, to educate and train them. This must be met, and we must carry right through the truth of God at any cost. We understand something about it, but there are many who do not understand anything about it, therefore we need to lead them along, to i**nstruct them kindly and tenderly**, and if the Spirit of God is with us, we will know just what to say. "
>
> *EVANGELISM*, PAGE 339

Sometimes new converts will make mistakes as they attempt to share their faith. They may say too much too soon. As we instruct them to share first what Jesus has done for them, their witness will touch hearts.

STEP 10: INVITE NEW BELIEVERS TO JOIN A WITNESSING GROUP

Now these new believers are ready to **share their newfound faith** with others. Invite them to join the *Soup & Salvation* program. Some will be involved in prayer ministry, while others will go out and distribute literature and Bible enrollment cards. Others will use their spiritual gift of teaching; they will be involved in giving Bible studies. Invite them to join any outreach group that would best suit their gifts and talents.

PRACTICAL IDEAS

❦ Get them involved in one of the *Soup & Salvation* ministries:

- ❑ Prayer ministry
- ❑ Literature ministry
- ❑ Visitation ministry
- ❑ Bible study ministry

❦ Get them involved in:

- ❑ Home Bible seminar ministry
- ❑ Health ministry
- ❑ Children's ministry
- ❑ Any other outreach ministry

> "The **best medicine you can give the church** is not preaching or sermonizing, but **planning work for them**. If set to work, the despondent would soon forget their despondency, the weak would become strong, the ignorant intelligent, and all would be prepared to present the truth as it is in Jesus."
>
> *EVANGELISM*, PAGE 356

This **follow-up strategy** blends continuing doctrinal **Bible studies, personal devotions, social fellowship** and an involvement in **witnessing**. This provides an opportunity for the new converts to share challenges they face as well as prayer requests.

As you implement these principles, the Holy Spirit will help you to grow strong disciples for Christ. New converts will mature into solid Christians. Some will become leaders in your church. Many will actively share their faith with their relatives and friends.

As a rock thrown into a pond sends ripples across the water, the influence of this after-care program will have a ripple effect on scores of lives. *Only eternity will reveal its lasting influence.*

APPENDIX A

THE INTEREST FILE

The interest file is like a garden with plants at varying stages of development. Some are like seeds that have just been planted. They have not yet sprouted, yet they are silently growing. Other interests are like plants that have just begun to grow. Then there are interests that are like ripe fruit. They are ready to pick—ready for the harvest.

Like any garden, the interest file needs care. When it is carefully worked and properly cultivated it will produce an abundant harvest.

The interest file is one of the soul-winner's best friends. When you understand how to organize, evaluate and work your interest file, you will regularly discover new precious interests for Jesus.

DEVELOPING AN INTEREST FILE

Names in the interest file should include those the pastor and church members have secured from a variety of sources, such as:

- Those attending church and Sabbath School who are not baptized
- Those attending church who signed the visitor registration
- Those who have attended previous evangelistic meetings
- Friends and relatives of Seventh-day Adventists
- Those who have taken Bible studies
- Former church members

- *It Is Written Television* contacts
- *Voice of Prophecy* radio contacts
- All media contacts
- Literature distribution contacts
- Those who have attended cooking schools and other health programs
- Community service contacts
- Religious survey interests
- Vacation Bible School contacts

GETTING NAMES FOR VISITATION

- Develop an interest file by entering all names from the above sources on a computerized list.
- Appoint an interest information secretary to keep your interest file up to date.
- Once you begin your visitation program, you should go through the file and categorize your interests as A, B, or C.

A—B—C—INTEREST BASICS

"A" Interests

- People attending church
- People studying the Bible, attending a Bible class or preparing for baptism

"B" Interests

- Former church members who still believe the Adventist message
- Relatives of church members who believe the message, but are not taking Bible studies or attending church
- Those who visit the church occasionally
- *It Is Written, Voice of Prophecy, Faith for Today, La Voz, Amazing Facts, Breath of Life, Quiet Hour* or other media interests
- Those who have attended evangelistic meetings

"C" Interests

- Contacts of church members
- Health program attendees
- Literature and community service contacts
- Religious survey interests

Note: As you visit it is important to continually grade the interests. All "B" interests can be turned very quickly into "A" interests. Depending on circumstances, a "C" interest can move up very quickly to become a "B" or even an "A" interest.

CODING INTERESTS

Coding all the interests provides your visitation teams with important information. The following is a sample code for sources of interests.

A—B—C—INTERESTS

"A" INTERESTS – It is very important to work with "A" interests immediately. The goal for the "A" interests is to begin systematic Bible studies. Concentrate on leading those already in regular Bible studies to progressive decisions. It is important to code all interests for effective visitation.

CODE:
AC Attending church
ABC Attending Bible class
BS Bible studies

"B" INTERESTS – The goal with "B" interests is to develop relationships through visitation and lead them into regular Bible studies. This can be done effectively as the visitation and Bible study ministry teams visit.

CODE:
BSDA Backslidden Seventh-day Adventist
ISDA Inactive Seventh-day Adventist
FSDA Friend of Seventh-day Adventist
RSDA Relative of Seventh-day Adventist
AEM Attended evangelistic meetings
DBS *Discover* Bible School
IIW *It Is Written Television*
VOP *Voice Of Prophecy* radio
BOL *Breath of Life* television
FFT *Faith for Today* television
AF *Amazing Facts* television and radio
QH *Quiet Hour* radio
3ABN Three Angels Broadcasting Network
LAVOZ *La Voz* radio

"C" INTERESTS – "C" interests are usually more casual contacts. However, people can progress from a "C" interest to an "A" interest rapidly. Changing circumstances in life often create an openness to the gospel. Visit and watch for the openings.

CODE:
LE Literature evangelist (contacts)
VBS Vacation Bible School (contacts)
HP Health program (contacts)
CS Community service (contacts)
CC Casual contacts

Note: There may be some form of outreach that we have not included here. If there is, add it and choose a code. The key is to keep it simple.

CULTIVATING THE INTEREST FILE

Suggestions for cultivating the interest file

1. Mail a series of four systematic mailings to each name in the interest file. (See sample letters on the following pages.)

2. Call each interest in the interest file and do the telephone survey. (See Page 136)

INTEREST FILE LETTERS

The following letters can be mailed systematically to your interest list to develop active interests. Each letter makes a different offer. The first offers a free Bible course, *Search for Certainty*. The second offers a free book. We have used the book *To Hope Again* by Mark Finley. The third is an invitation to attend the *Unsealing Daniel's Mysteries* seminar and the fourth is an invitation to attend an evangelistic series. We normally mail these letters quarterly, tying them to the appropriate scheduled events in our evangelistic countdown calendar.

Note: The sample letters that follow are just that—samples. Please feel free to edit them in any way you wish to fit your local situation and particular needs. But each sample, as it stands, will give you a good start and may, in fact, be used with minimum changes. Insert the *Search for Certainty* Bible enrollment card with this letter.

Dear Friend,

What an exciting time to be alive! We have entered into the 21ST century. Ours is a generation that blends optimism regarding the future with serious concern. We are optimistic about society's technological advances with new breakthroughs in health care and disease control. But we are also concerned about waning moral values, the rapid deterioration of the family unit, and rampant sex and violence on television. Electrical energy shortages, an uncertain economy, rising crime and natural disasters trouble us. Is there anything certain? What can we really hang on to in a time of crisis?

Many people are finding answers in *It Is Written Television's* new set of *Search for Certainty* Bible guides authored by Mark Finley.

If ever there was a time to seek answers to the deepest questions of the human heart, it is today. If ever there was a time to understand the Bible for ourselves, it is today. The *Search for Certainty* lessons make Bible study fascinating and easy to understand. These lessons will answer such questions as: What does the Bible teach about the end times? What are the signs of the coming of Jesus? How can I get answers to my prayers? What happens when you die? What is heaven really like? These and many other questions will be answered as you personally explore the great teachings of Scripture.

These lessons are yours absolutely free. There is no cost. Your only commitment is to faithfully complete the lessons. If you would like to deepen your faith by participating in this Bible study adventure, **mail the enclosed card today**. You will understand answers to questions you have asked all of your life. We will be delighted to deliver your lessons immediately upon receiving your card. Be assured you are poised on the verge of thrilling new discoveries that will bring you greater peace of mind, deeper joy and meaning in your life.

Sincerely your friend,

Dear Friend,

Occasionally I come across a book that brings me such inspiration that I want to share it. Recently, I read *To Hope Again* by my good friend, Mark Finley, of *It Is Written Television*. This small volume outlines the great prophetic chapters of the Bible, focusing especially on the second coming of Christ. It is filled with hope. It describes the signs of Christ's soon return as well as how to prepare for the second coming of Christ.

Each chapter is a description of the events that will occur in connection with the second coming of Christ. This book will give you insight into what is coming upon the world. It is yours absolutely free. I will be delighted to present it to you as a gift. I am personally convinced that we are living in the days when Bible prophecy is being fulfilled.

This book will help you prepare for the events that will soon take place in our world. Our loving Lord desires you to be ready for His return. He desires that your family meet Him in peace and live with Him forever. This book, *To Hope Again,* will provide you with inspiration, hope and courage.

Please mail the enclosed card today to receive your free copy of *To Hope Again*. We will deliver your book immediately.

Sincerely in Christ,

FREE BOOK OFFER

❑ Yes, I'd like a copy of *To Hope Again* at no cost or obligation.
Please deliver my free book to:

NAME ____________________

ADDRESS ____________________

CITY ____________________

STATE __________ ZIP __________

TO HOPE AGAIN

Mark Finley
with Steve Mosley

Note: The mailing address on the card should be the mailing address of the local church –or– *(preferably)* a post office box with a Bible school name and address.

Dear Friend,

I would like to give you a personal invitation to attend the *Unsealing Daniel's Mysteries* seminar.

History has been following Daniel's prophecies like a blueprint. For 2,500 years, these prophecies have been unfolding. Daniel's prophecies named kings, rulers and empires before their appearance in history.

During this 12-session seminar we will cover such topics as:

- The future of the world
- How to survive tough times
- How to discover truth
- How to be ready for the coming of Christ
- When church and state unite
- The truth about the end time
- The longest time prophecy in the Bible and many more topics

I have enclosed a brochure for the *Unsealing Daniel's Mysteries* seminar. Be sure to attend and receive 12 free lessons on the prophetic themes of Daniel that contain charts, diagrams and supplementary material.

During the *Unsealing Daniel's Mysteries* seminar, you will see the prophecies of Daniel come to life. You can review the lessons at home as you study the Bible prophecies of Daniel. You will be among the many who are saying, "I never knew Bible prophecy could be so clear."

Tens of thousands testify that these prophecies have changed their lives. Be sure to attend the *Unsealing Daniel's Mysteries* seminar that begins:

Date:
Time:
Location:

It Is Written Television is sponsoring the *Unsealing Daniel's Mysteries* seminar. There is no charge. I look forward to seeing you there.

Sincerely your friend,

Dear Friend,

Here's some good news you will not want to miss. Mark Finley, the speaker for *It Is Written Television,* will be conducting a series of meetings on Bible prophecy via video, titled *Revelation of Hope. Revelation of Hope* has been conducted around the world to packed audiences. Tens of thousands have appreciated his dynamic presentations on the Bible's last book, Revelation.

During this hope-filled series, you will learn more than you ever have in your life on Revelation's end-time prophecies. You will discover answers to such questions as:

- Who is the beast?
- What does the mysterious number 666 mean?
- What and where is the Battle of Armageddon?
- What do Revelation's mysterious symbols mean?
- Who are the four horsemen of the Revelation?
- What is America's role in Bible prophecy?
- Does the Bible predict 1,000 years of peace?

Discover for yourself God's outline for the future. You can face the future with new confidence. *Revelation of Hope* is a gripping multimedia presentation that will hold your attention from the first minute of the program until the end.

We have enclosed a colorful brochure describing the program in detail. We also have a free place reserved especially for you. To make your reservation, please call 000-0000.

We look forward to seeing you at the *Revelation of Hope* Bible prophecy series beginning ___________(date), at________________. Join the thousands who testify that, "This is the most powerful, hope-filled, presentation I have ever attended!"

Sincerely,

APPENDIX B

PRINCIPLES IN CONTACTING FORMER SEVENTH-DAY ADVENTISTS

Christ spent a good share of His ministry trying to reach those who strayed from the fold. In Luke 15 He gave three parables to teach a lesson to the religious leaders of His day. These religious leaders taught that God rejoiced when a sinner or backslider was destroyed. Christ showed through these three parables that God is waiting for the lost to be found. He is anxious and waiting to reclaim them and bring them back to the fold. He said that there is rejoicing in heaven when one lost sinner is found.

> "'For this my son was dead and is alive again; he was lost and is found.' And they began to be merry. 'It was right that we should make merry and be glad, for your brother was dead and is alive again, and was lost and is found.'"
>
> *LUKE 15:24, 32*

In the last days of earth's history, many who are lost will come back to Christ. It is our responsibility to rescue those who once believed, but who have gone astray.

> "When the storm of persecution really breaks upon us, the true sheep will hear the true Shepherd's voice. Self-denying efforts will be put forth to save the lost, and many who have strayed from the fold will come back to follow the great Shepherd."
>
> *EVANGELISM*, PAGE 693

When working with former Seventh-day Adventists, it is important to understand why they have left the church, as well as principles for bringing them back to the fold.

UNDERSTANDING WHY SEVENTH-DAY ADVENTISTS LEAVE THE CHURCH

1. The perception that the Church is no longer relevant in their life and does not meet their needs

- Most people do not leave the Seventh-day Adventist Church because they no longer believe the doctrines. Many believe the Adventist Church has the truth for this day. Even if they are not living in accordance with God's standards, they still have the conviction about the correctness of the major beliefs of the church.

• Some church members have never been assimilated into the church family.

• They have a growing disinterest in spiritual things in general, due to a lack of adequate devotional and Bible study life.

2. Deep, personal tragedy

• Often they have gone through some deep, personal tragedy. Their spiritual lives have eroded.

• They have had a conflict with the pastor or some other church member. Many former Adventists can be reclaimed through personal visitation when there is genuine concern.

3. Discouragement with themselves over a failure to live in harmony with church standards

• Many former Seventh-day Adventists have something they feel is too great for God to forgive. They feel they have gone too far, that God is not willing to forgive them. Of course, this is not true. We must be positive in our presentation of God's willingness to forgive and His great desire to have them return to Him.

• Many feel guilty because they have not been living in harmony with church standards. Some have gone back to smoking or drinking. Some have gone through a divorce. Some have been working on the Bible Sabbath. They need someone who cares about them and is ready and willing to help them live the victorious life they long to have.

PRINCIPLES TO FOLLOW WHEN CONTACTING FORMER SEVENTH-DAY ADVENTIST CHURCH MEMBERS

1. Spend time in prayer before you visit former Seventh-day Adventist church members. Ask God for wisdom.

2. At the door, identify yourself as a member of the local Seventh-day Adventist Church.

EXAMPLE:

"Hello, my name is ______________ and this is my friend ____________. We are from the ____________ Seventh-day Adventist Church. We just stopped by to let you know about some of the exciting events happening at the church. We also wanted to give you this book and let you know we care about you." (Use the Pacific Press sharing book, *Satisfied*.)

3. Once they invite you inside, demonstrate love, acceptance and genuine concern.

4. Begin your conversation with topics of general interest such as:

• "Have you lived in this community for a number of years?" (Carefully notice any clues around the house that may indicate their interest in spiritual things.)

• "Are you married? Do you have children?"

• "Do you work close to home? What is your occupation?"

5. Proceed to topics of religious interest by asking such questions as the following ones:
   - "I understand you used to attend the Seventh-day Adventist Church regularly. Is that correct?"
   - "How long ago was that?"
   - "How did you happen to join the church?"

6. Listen carefully. Ask questions.
Do not pass judgment on either the individual or the church. Make a comment like,
   - "I can understand why you might feel that way!"

7. After listening carefully, share what Jesus Christ means to you. Describe His incredible mercy, His marvelous forgiveness and His power to change lives.

8. Don't criticize or appear shocked at any aspect of their lifestyle. Listen carefully. Certainly don't take sides in any personal conflict they have had. Simply express your regret or sorrow over their pain.

9. Invite them to a social event, holiday program, health series or Bible seminar. Ask if you can visit again.

10. Concentrate on building a friendship.

As we lovingly reach out to former or inactive Adventists, the Spirit of God will minister through us to touch their hearts. Many will be won to Christ. Many will return. God will touch their hearts. You can be used by God to bring them back.

What a joy it will be when they come back to Christ!

APPENDIX C

CONVERSATIONAL PRAYER

WHAT IS CONVERSATIONAL PRAYER?

❦ Conversational prayer happens when two or more people have a conversation with God—when they talk to God as we do to each other.

❦ We pray about various subjects together by topic. All participants are pursuing the same topic until all who want to pray about it have the opportunity to do so before moving on to another topic.

❦ One person begins the prayer by addressing God, so there is no need for each person to address God; and no formal ending is needed until it is time to close the prayer session. The person who starts the prayer session usually ends it, although they can pray several times before closure.

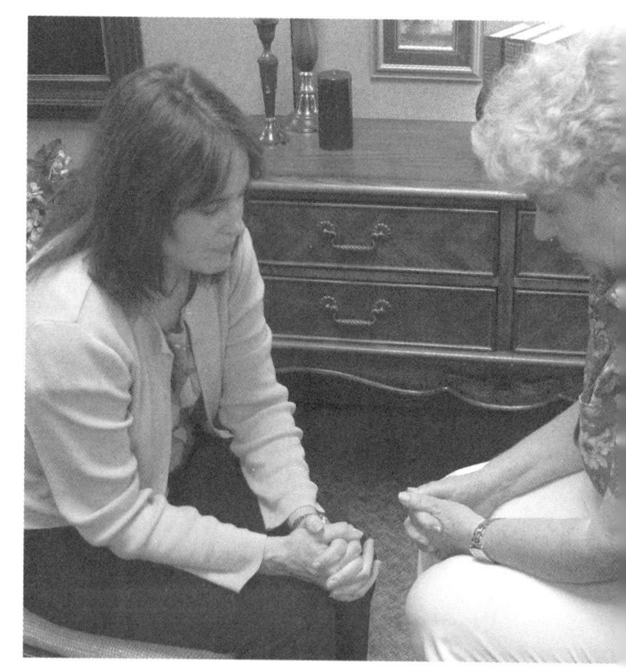

❦ Each person may pray as many times as he wants as long as it is on the same subject. This type of prayer is like having a conversation with a friend. There is no need to pray around the circle—everyone may pray as impressed by the Spirit.

❦ When we pray we are aware of the prayers of others. We need to be in tune with their feelings and needs. We do this by staying on the same subject and affirming their prayer. Let all those who want to affirm the subject do so before going on to another subject.

❦ It is important to use simple sentences, not more than a couple at one time. We are not making speeches to God or to others. We are just talking to Him as we do to each other. Make your prayer short so others have the opportunity to pray.

❦ If you have several things you want to thank God for, do it several times rather than all at one time.

HERE ARE SOME PRACTICAL SUGGESTIONS TO MAKE CONVERSATIONAL PRAYER MORE EFFECTIVE.

1. Pray—Avoid spending the entire time in a study group or on a lesson

- This is the quickest way to squeeze out prayer.
- The study of *Prayer Warriors,* or Scripture such as the book of Acts, should be

a catalyst to prayer.

• The prayer time is the most important aspect of the evening. It is in prayer that we genuinely seek God's power in witness.

2. Plan a conclusion time

• Just as there is a point of beginning, there should be a time for completion. Prayer time should last approximately 45-50 minutes (not longer than an hour.)

3. Get comfortable in a circle

• If necessary to facilitate comfort, bring a pillow. It is important that discomfort not distract from the spirit of prayer.

• It takes time to develop a prayer experience. It will be necessary to stay on our knees for a while for something to happen.

• Focused praying taps into the power of God. Spasmodic, half-hearted praying produces few results.

4. Get close enough so all can hear

• It is best to keep the group no larger than 20-25, or else the group may become scattered and participants will feel uninvolved.

• We often divide into groups of 8-12 so each person has a better opportunity to participate.

5. Use short-sentence prayers

• Each person does not need to readdress God as he begins to pray. All prayers are part of the whole. When the last person prays, he should conclude the prayer with "Amen."

6. Affirm each preceding prayer

• Before continuing with a new thought, it is important that at least one or two persons affirm (agree with) the prayer of the one who has just prayed. This is what Jesus was speaking of when He said, "If two of you shall agree on earth as touching anything that they shall ask, it shall be done for them by My Father in Heaven." (Matthew 18:19)

7. Change the atmosphere by song

• Periodically, intersperse prayers with songs such as "Whisper a Prayer," "Thank You, Lord for Saving My Soul," "Father, I Adore You," "Into My Heart," etc. This will help to keep the prayers vibrant.

8. Pray with thanksgiving

• Thanksgiving is a good way to begin, thus giving everyone an opportunity to thank God for a single blessing. Praise and thank Him for the blessings He has given you. If you have several blessings you want to thank God for, do it several times rather than all at once.

You are in for a wonderful new experience as you enter into conversational prayer with our Lord!

APPENDIX D

IT IS WRITTEN
SURVEY APPROACH

"Good afternoon, I am __________________ and this is my friend __________________. We represent *It Is Written Television*. We appreciate the fact that you have been viewing our program and have requested some of our inspirational books. Mark Finley, speaker for the telecast, has asked us to call our viewers to ask for their suggestions about the program. May I take two minutes of your time to ask just a few brief survey questions? This will help us make the program even better."

1. How often do you watch the *It Is Written* program?

   ❑ Regularly ❑ Occasionally ❑ Seldom

2. Which of the program topics listed below would interest you most?

   ❑ a. Health (Vegetarianism, stress reduction, etc.)
   ❑ b. Family (Marriage, parent/child relationships)
   ❑ c. The Christian Life (Prayer, Bible study, faith, etc.)
   ❑ d. Bible Prophecy (Daniel/Revelation)
   ❑ e. Bible Doctrines (Death, second coming, salvation, finding truth)
   ❑ f. Current Events (What's really behind what is going on in the world)
   ❑ g. Archaeology (How discoveries in the Middle East confirm the Bible)

3. If you could suggest any topic for Pastor Finley to speak about, what would it be?

Answer: ____

4. Pastor Finley has been offering Bible study lessons. Have you heard about these new lessons called *Search for Certainty*?

   ❑ Yes ❑ No

This is the end of the survey. You can then say,

"Thank you so much for your helpful answers to our survey. This information will be passed on to *It Is Written* to help in their future programming. Pastor Finley would like to invite you to enjoy a sample of free Bible study lessons. You can just fill out this Bible enrollment card, and someone will come by and drop off the lessons. We appreciate your time. Have a wonderful day."

NOTE: This can be used either as a visitation or telephone survey for It Is Written viewers.

APPENDIX E

IT IS WRITTEN DOOR-TO-DOOR BOOK APPROACH

The following is a sample of what you could say at the door as you follow up *It Is Written* interests when delivering a book and introducing them to the *Search for Certainty* Bible lessons.

"Hello, my name is ______________________ and this is my friend ______________________.
We are representatives from *It Is Written Television.* We just wanted to let you know how excited we are that you are watching the *It Is Written* telecast. Pastor Finley asked that we give you one of his latest books. Have you seen this book before?" **(Wait for response)**

"We hope you will enjoy it. We also wanted to let you know that Pastor Finley is offering a new series of Bible studies called *Search for Certainty.* Do you like studying the Bible?" **(Wait for response)**

"Many people today have a great interest in Bible study, but they wonder how to begin a systematic study on their own. These lessons will lead you through different Bible topics. You will notice that all the answers are found in the Scriptures. I know these lessons will enrich your personal life and will lead you to a deeper relationship with Christ. Is this something that would interest you?" **(Wait for response)**

"Great! We'll leave the first lesson with you today. Simply read the notes, ask the questions and find the answers in the Bible. We'd be happy to come by next week at this time to see how you've done and drop off a couple more lessons, if that would be convenient for you." **(Wait for response)**

"Thank you for visiting with us today." **(Wait for response)**

"Could we have a short prayer with you before we leave?" (Pray)

"See you next week, God bless you!"

Note: If the person says, "Oh, I thought these would be coming in the mail," just respond by saying:

"A number of people have thought that. However, we find that many appreciate some direction in doing the lessons, so that's why we have come. If you prefer to do them by mail we do have a correspondence school."

(At this point introduce them to the *Discover* lessons. Share with them the details of how the correspondence school works.)

APPENDIX F

COMMUNITY RELIGIOUS SURVEY

There will be Bible study contacts found from a community religious survey that you may not find any other way. The following are some important things to keep in mind as you conduct door-to-door surveys.

SUPPLIES NEEDED

- Clipboard and pen
- Survey forms
- Brochures (for various programs such as the cooking school, Daniel seminar, *Revelation of Hope* or *New Beginnings* evangelistic series)
- Magazines (such as *Peace Above the Storm)* with Bible enrollment cards

ANSWER THREE BASIC QUESTIONS

When you knock on a door, most people have three questions. It is important to answer these questions immediately.

- "Who are you?"
- "Why are you here?"
- "How long will you stay?"

WHAT TO SAY

"Hello, my name is ______________________ and this is my friend ______________________. We're conducting a community religious survey in the area sponsored by *It Is Written Television.* Could we take just a few moments of your time to ask you four simple questions?"

Ask the community religious survey questions. After you have completed the questions, make the transition which follows at the bottom of the survey.

COMMUNITY RELIGIOUS SURVEY

1. Do you have a church preference?

❑ Catholic
❑ Baptist
❑ Church of God
❑ Lutheran
❑ Jehovah's Witness
❑ Adventist
❑ Presbyterian
❑ Pentecostal
❑ Methodist
❑ Jewish
❑ Mormon
❑ Other

2. Do you attend church?

❑ Regularly
❑ Occasionally
❑ Almost never
❑ Never

3. Do you believe that if the Bible were read and followed, it would solve the problems of crime in our society?

❑ YES ❑ NO

4. If there were four lectures being held in town tonight which one would interest you the most?

❑ Money/Finances
❑ Health
❑ Basic Bible study
❑ Bible prophecy

"Thank you for participating in the survey. In appreciation for the time you have taken to answer these questions, we would like to give you this magazine. Included with the magazine is a Bible enrollment card for a series of free Bible studies. You can send it in anytime you wish. Thank you again and God bless you."

APPENDIX F

SURVEY MATERIALS

Below are samples of suggested materials to have available for distribution during community surveys.

APPENDIX G

YOURS FOR THE ASKING

We want to help you achieve life's greatest happiness.
Please check the items below that interest you the most.

❑ I would like a complimentary copy of *Radiant Living Magazine* (*Simple Steps to Health and Happiness.*)

❑ Please place my name on your mailing list for upcoming health programs.

❑ I am interested in attending the following classes:

- ❑ *Natural Lifestyle Cooking*
- ❑ Stress management
- ❑ Stop-smoking program
- ❑ Family life series
- ❑ Prophecy seminar emphasizing the Bible book of Daniel titled, *Unsealing Daniel's Mysteries.*

❑ I am interested in more information about becoming a part of an informal Bible study group.

❑ I would like an absolutely free series of Bible study lessons.

❑ I am interested in studying prophecy by watching videotapes.

Name ______________________

Address ______________________

City ______________ State ______ Zip ______

Telephone ( ) ______________________

E-Mail Address ______________________

APPENDIX H

REGISTRATION FORM

LIGHT YOUR WORLD FOR GOD TRAINING CLASS

Name ______________________________

Address ______________________________

City ______________ State ______ Zip ______

Home Phone (   ) ______________ Work Phone (   ) ______________

E-Mail ______________________________

Church ______________________________

______ Initial this line to indicate you have received the *Light Your World for God* manual.

Please answer the following questions. This will let us know where we can be the most help.

1. I have previously attended a Bible study ministry training class. ❑ YES ❑ NO

2. If so, how long ago did you attend? ______ Month(s) ago ________ Year(s) ago

3. I have given Bible studies.

   ❑ Never
   ❑ Occasionally
   ❑ Regularly

4. Write the name of the series of lessons you have used or are using.

____

____

5. How many people are you currently studying the Bible with?

____

APPENDIX I

HOME BIBLE SEMINAR
REGISTRATION FORM
UNSEALING DANIEL'S MYSTERIES

LEADER ______________________________

ADDRESS ______________________________

CITY ______________ STATE ______ ZIP ______

HOME PHONE ______________________________

WORK PHONE ______________________________

CELL PHONE ______________________________

E-MAIL ______________________________

CO-LEADER ______________________________

ADDRESS ______________________________

CITY ______________ STATE ______ ZIP ______

HOME PHONE ______________________________

WORK PHONE ______________________________

CELL PHONE ______________________________

E-MAIL ______________________________

PARTICIPANT ______________________________

PARTICIPANT ______________________________

PARTICIPANT ______________________________

PARTICIPANT ______________________________

PARTICIPANT ______________________________

APPENDIX J

REQUEST FORM FOR
MEDIA MINISTRY NAMES

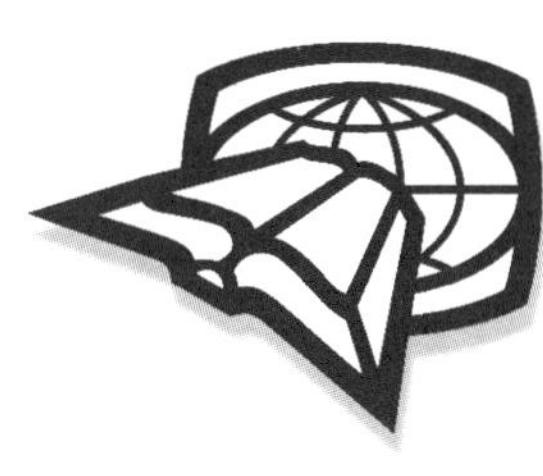

Please return this form at least six weeks before your meetings to:

It Is Written
Attn: Opal Mitchell
101 W. Cochran Street
Simi Valley, CA 93065

Or fax to: 805-955-7734
To call dial: 805-955-7741

FOR OFFICE USE ONLY:
DATE RECEIVED ______
DATE TO MAIL ______

It Is Written	❏ Names and addresses	❏ Labels	❏ Letters of invitation
Voice of Prophecy	❏ Names and addresses	❏ Labels	❏ Letters of invitation
Faith for Today	❏ Names and addresses	❏ Labels	(No letters available)
La Voz (Spanish)	❏ Names and addresses	❏ Labels	❏ Letters of invitation

Note: The letters of invitation will be signed by each ministry's speaker and sent out from the ministry using first class mail rate. You will be charged for postage. There is a $10 cover charge for any or all services requested. The $10 fee will be billed to your address. If you are requesting letters of invitation to be sent, please fill in #1-10. If you are requesting names and addresses or labels, please fill in #10 only.

1. Location of evangelistic series/seminar—City: ______ State: ______
2. Name of meeting place: ______
3. Street address of meeting place: ______
4. Date of first meeting: ______ Meeting time—Hour: ______ Days of week: S M T W T F S
5. Name of speaker: ______
6. Title of opening presentation: ______
7. Telephone number for more information: ______
8. Special features: ❏ Childcare ❏ Children's meetings ❏ Music ❏ Visuals
9. Do you wish handbills to be included in each letter of invitation? ❏ Yes ❏ No

   (If yes, please fold to fit 4 x 9 envelope and send to us four weeks prior to evangelistic meetings to include with letter.)
10. Zip codes from which names are to be selected (please list below)

Zip codes	Zip codes	Zip codes	Zip codes

Submitted by (Name): ______
Church/Organization for Billing ______
Address ______
Shipping Address (if different from above) ______
City ______ State ______ Zip ______
Home Phone ( ) ______ Church Phone ( ) ______
E-Mail ______

APPENDIX K

SEARCH FOR CERTAINTY

BIBLE ENROLLMENT CARDS
FOLLOWING UP AND DELIVERING BIBLE LESSONS

The *Search for Certainty* Bible study cards are mailed throughout your community. When they come back to the local church, they need to be followed up and the Bible lessons should be delivered. The following instructions can be helpful in getting a Bible study started.

First, when you knock on someone's door, the person on the other side wants to know three basic things:

- "Who is it?"
- "What do you want?"
- "How long are you going to stay?"

You can answer those questions in the first two minutes at the door.

"Hello, my name is ________________and this is my friend ________________. We are from *It Is Written Television,* which is sponsoring the Bible study program. We recently received your card." (Have their card in your hand and show it to them.)

"We are delighted that you are interested in the study of the Bible. You requested the Bible study guides and we have them here to give you as a free gift. May I take just a few minutes to explain how to complete them?"

In less than two minutes, you have told them who you are, where you are from and why you are there. Then, addressing the person by name, say:

"You know Mrs. ________________, in the world we live in, it is easy to have a lot of questions about life. Some people wonder what happens when a person dies, or whether the world will be destroyed by nuclear war. Others wonder why there is so much suffering.

"I've discovered that most people have a Bible, but they don't know how to study it, and oftentimes it can be confusing to them. These simple Bible guides will help to answer some of life's greatest questions and make the Bible easy to understand. Like a lot of other people, you may be concerned about crime, world war or all the natural disasters taking place.

"The first lesson is on the truthfulness of the Bible and how the Bible contains life-changing principles which can lead to a happier life.

"We'll leave these two lessons with you and you can complete them at your leisure this week. Do you have a Bible that you can study from or would you like me to loan this one to you? After you complete 15 of the lessons we will give you the Bible as a gift."

At this point it is important to show the people how to do the lessons.

Take out Lesson #1 and show the student how to look up the texts and answer the questions. People will take the lessons, but when you return the second time, they often won't have them done. They will just hand them back to you. We risk giving up on a lot of people too soon because they don't fill in their lessons; the real problem is that they simply don't know how. It is vital on this first visit to take time to show them how to fill in the lessons. This should only take about 10 minutes.

Take them through at least the first three questions.

"Would it be all right with you if we came back next week at this time to see how you have done with the lessons and drop off a couple more lessons for you to do?"

Before leaving, ask the person if you could have a simple prayer with them to ask God to bless them as they do the lessons.

"Dear Lord, thank you for Mrs. _______________, who has a desire to study the Bible. Help her as she opens your word to understand more fully your plan for the future and how you are leading in her own life. Please bless her and guide her, Amen.

"I look forward to seeing you again next week. Good-bye."

Note: There will be some people who will say, "Oh, I expected the lessons to come through the mail."
At this point explain why you are dropping the lessons off in person.

"There are some who think the lessons are coming in the mail, but many find it a little difficult to do the lessons without someone explaining how to do them, so we like to come by in person to explain how it's done."

Watch their response. If the person shows some resistance to having you come to their home, say:

"However, we do have a correspondence school for those who would rather have them delivered by mail."

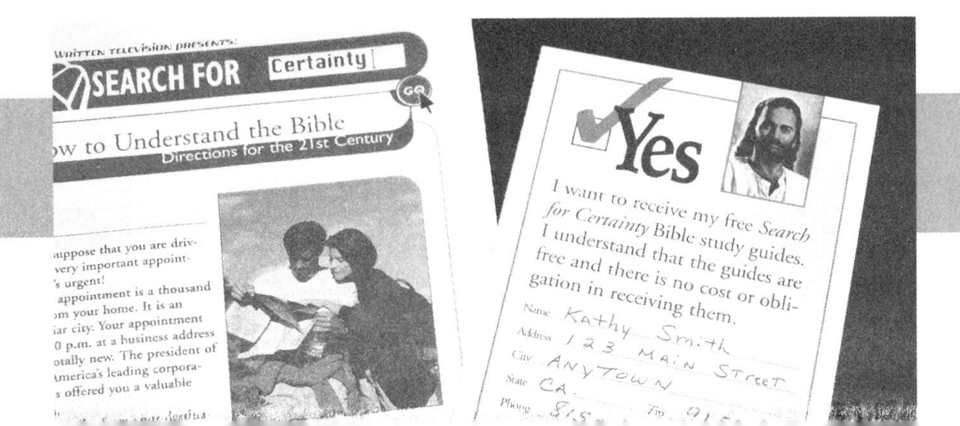

APPENDIX L — TOPIC AND BIBLICAL REFERENCE

SEARCH FOR CERTAINTY Bible Lessons

LESSON	TITLE	TOPIC	BIBLICAL REFERENCE
1	**HOW TO UNDERSTAND THE BIBLE** DIRECTIONS FOR THE 21ST CENTURY	INTRODUCTION LESSON ON HOW TO STUDY THE BIBLE	
2	**OUR DAY IN THE LIGHT OF BIBLE PROPHECY** CERTAINTY FOR THE 21ST CENTURY	WORLD HISTORY REVIEW	DANIEL 2
3	**A WORLD IN TURMOIL** CONFIDENCE FOR THE 21ST CENTURY	SIGNS OF THE TIMES	MATTHEW 24 AND SELECTED PASSAGES FROM REVELATION
4	**THE MANNER OF CHRIST'S COMING** HOPE FOR THE 21ST CENTURY	SECOND COMING	SELECTED PASSAGES THROUGHOUT SCRIPTURE, INCLUDING REVELATION
5	**HOW TO FIND PERSONAL PEACE** PEACE FOR THE 21ST CENTURY	SALVATION	
6	**THE SECRET OF A NEW LIFE** POWER FOR LIVING IN THE 21ST CENTURY	DIVINITY OF CHRIST	SELECTED PASSAGES ON PROPHECIES OF THE MESSIAH
7	**GOOD GOD! BAD WORLD! WHY?** MAKING SENSE OF EVIL IN THE 21ST CENTURY	ORIGIN OF EVIL	REVELATION 12
8	**REVELATION'S MOST THRILLING MESSAGE** AN END-TIME MESSAGE FOR THE 21ST CENTURY	THREE ANGELS' MESSAGE, INTRODUCTION	REVELATION 14
9	**THE BIBLE'S LONGEST & MOST AMAZING PROPHECY** GODLY LIVING IN THE 21ST CENTURY	THE JUDGMENT	REVELATION 14 AND DANIEL 8-9
10	**A DATE WITH DESTINY: THE JUDGMENT** CHOICES IN THE 21ST CENTURY	THE NATURE OF THE JUDGMENT	DANIEL 7
11	**WHAT'S BEHIND RISING CRIME, VIOLENCE AND IMMORALITY?** A STANDARD FOR THE 21ST CENTURY	THE LAW	EMPHASIS ON REVELATION 11
12	**CHRIST'S SPECIAL SIGN** REST FOR THE RESTLESS IN THE 21ST CENTURY	SABBATH	REVELATION 4 AND REVELATION 14
13	**TAMPERING WITH HEAVEN'S CONSTITUTION** HONESTY FOR THE 21ST CENTURY	CHANGE OF THE SABBATH	DANIEL 7
14	**MODERN CULTS IDENTIFIED FIVE WAYS** AVOIDING DECEPTION IN THE 21ST CENTURY	UNDERSTANDING TRUTH	SELECTED PASSAGES THROUGHOUT SCRIPTURE WITH SPECIAL EMPHASIS ON REVELATION
15	**OUR GREATEST NEED–NEW LIFESTYLE!** HEALTH IN THE 21ST CENTURY	HEALTH	A UNIQUE APPROACH FROM REVELATION 14:6-7
16	**THE REAL TRUTH ABOUT DEATH** HOPE BEYOND THE GRAVE IN THE 21ST CENTURY	STATE OF THE DEAD	SELECTED PASSAGES THROUGHOUT SCRIPTURE WITH EMPHASIS ON REVELATION 14:13
17	**GOD'S LOVE IN THE FIRES OF HELL** TRIUMPH IN THE 21ST CENTURY	DESTRUCTION OF THE WICKED	SELECTED PASSAGES THROUGHOUT SCRIPTURE WITH EMPHASIS ON REVELATION 14 AND 20
18	**HOW TO SUCCESSFULLY BURY THE PAST** NEW LIFE IN THE 21ST CENTURY	BAPTISM	
19	**A FINANCIAL SECRET** WISE INVESTMENT IN THE 21ST CENTURY	TITHE	
20	**GROWING AS A CHRISTIAN** PRACTICAL CHRISTIANITY FOR THE 21ST CENTURY	THE CHRISTIAN LIFE, PRAYER AND BIBLE STUDY	
21	**A MODERN-DAY MOVEMENT OF DESTINY** TRUTH FOR THE 21ST CENTURY	TRUE CHURCH	REVELATION 12
22	**PROPHETS AND PROPHECY/VISIONS AND DREAMS** INSIGHT FOR THE 21ST CENTURY	GIFT OF PROPHECY	REVELATION 12 AND REVELATION 19:10
23	**THE MYSTERY OF SPIRITUAL BABYLON REVEALED** GOD'S CALL FOR THE 21ST CENTURY	TRUTH VS. ERROR	REVELATION 17 AND 18
24	**HOLY SPIRIT AND UNPARDONABLE SIN** POWER FOR THE 21ST CENTURY	FOLLOWING TRUTH	
25	**THE SEARCH FOR CERTAINTY** A MOVEMENT FOR THE 21ST CENTURY	THE HISTORIC RISE OF THE TRUE CHURCH	REVELATION 10
26	**THE MARK OF THE BEAST AND THE MYSTERY NUMBER 666** A WARNING FOR THE 21ST CENTURY	LAST-DAY EVENTS	REV. 13:1-10 AND 16-18
27	**THE UNITED STATES IN BIBLE PROPHECY** LOYALTY FOR THE 21ST CENTURY	LAST-DAY EVENTS	REVELATION 13:11-16
28	**ARMAGEDDON AND THE SEVEN LAST PLAGUES** VICTORY FOR THE 21ST CENTURY	BATTLE OF ARMAGEDDON	REVELATION 16
29	**REVELATION PREDICTS 1,000-YEAR WORLD BLACKOUT** A NEW BEGINNING FOR THE 21ST CENTURY	MILLENNIUM	REVELATION 20
30	**REVELATION'S GLORIOUS CLIMAX** HOME FOR THE 21ST CENTURY	HEAVEN	REVELATION 21

APPENDIX M

BIBLE MARKING PLAN

FOR *SEARCH FOR CERTAINTY* BIBLE LESSONS

Some people find a Bible marking guide helpful for those occasions when they are called upon to give spontaneous Bible studies. The texts can easily be found by marking your Bible through the Bible Marking Plan. The system is simple and easy to follow. Marking your Bible also helps you answer questions even if there were no lessons available.

How to use the Bible Marking Plan:

1. Write the title of each *Search for Certainty* study in the back of your Bible with the first text next to it.

2. That text is then found in your Bible, and the second reference is written at the end of the passage. Continue with each following text in the study until the study is completed.

3. Each text then tells you where to go next. It will be helpful to circle the numbers of the texts used so that your eye will immediately catch the chapter and verse.

4. There will be a code with a key letter that identifies the subject of each study and appears before the number of the text. For example: B-2 would mean the second text in the study on the Bible. SC-3 would indicate the third text on the second coming of Christ.

Here is a code for the *Search for Certainty* Bible lessons.

1. **B**	Bible (Holy Bible)
2. **D2**	Our Day in the Light of Bible Prophecy (Daniel 2)
3. **ST**	A World in Turmoil (Signs of the times)
4. **MCC**	The Manner of Christ's Coming
5. **SAL**	How to Find Personal Peace (Salvation)
6. **GG**	The Secret of a New Life (God's grace)
7. **GC**	Good God! Bad World! Why? (Great controversy)
8. **3AM**	Revelation's Most Thrilling Message (Three Angels' Message)
9. **BLP**	The Bible's Longest and Most Amazing Prophecy (2,300 days)
10. **J**	A Date With Destiny (Judgment)
11. **L**	What's Behind Rising Crime, Violence and Immorality? (Law)
12. **S**	Christ's Special Sign (Sabbath)
13. **CS**	Tampering with Heaven's Constitution (Change of the Sabbath)
14. **C**	Modern Cults Identified Five Ways! (Cults)
15. **NL**	Our Greatest Need: New Lifestyle! (Health)
16. **D**	The Real Truth About Death (Death)
17. **HF**	God's Love in the Fires of Hell (Hellfire)
18. **BB**	How to Successfully Bury the Past (Bible baptism)
19. **T**	A Financial Secret (Tithe)
20. **GCE**	Growing as a Christian (Growing Christian experience)
21. **TC**	God's Church Identified (True church)
22. **SP**	Prophets and Prophecy/Visions and Dreams (Spirit of Prophecy)
23. **SBR**	The Mystery of Spiritual Babylon Revealed (Spiritual Babylon revealed)
24. **HS**	Holy Spirit and Unpardonable Sin
25. **DT**	From Disappointment to Triumph
26. **MB**	The Mark of the Beast and the Mystery Number 666
27. **US**	The United States in Prophecy
28. **SLP**	Armageddon and the Seven Last Plagues
29. **M**	Revelation Predicts 1,000-Year World Blackout (Millennium)
30. **H**	Revelation's Glorious Climax (Heaven)

APPENDIX N

SEARCH FOR CERTAINTY

BIBLE STUDY REGISTRATION FORM

Name of Bible Instructor

Phone (   )

E-Mail

Bible Student's Name

Address

City State Zip

Phone (   )

E-Mail

Source of Interest:

❑ Attending Church ❑ Friend ❑ *IIW*

❑ Bible Enrollment Card ❑ Relative of SDA ❑ *VOP*

❑ Other ____________________

Lessons Completed: Please **circle** lessons completed

1 2 3 4 5 6 7 8 9 10 11 12 13 14 15 16 17 18 19 20 21 22 23 24 25 26 27 28 29 30

Comments:

Baptized: ❑ No ❑ Yes Date:

Spiritual Guardian:

APPENDIX O

LIST OF BIBLE STUDENTS AND LESSONS COMPLETED

Please write full name (last name first) and address, and mark lessons completed.

No. NAME INSTRUCTOR

ADDRESS ZIP

1 2 3 4 5 6 7 8 9 10 11 12 13 14 15 16 17 18 19 20 21 22 23 24 25 26 27 28 29 30

No. NAME INSTRUCTOR

ADDRESS ZIP

1 2 3 4 5 6 7 8 9 10 11 12 13 14 15 16 17 18 19 20 21 22 23 24 25 26 27 28 29 30

No. NAME INSTRUCTOR

ADDRESS ZIP

1 2 3 4 5 6 7 8 9 10 11 12 13 14 15 16 17 18 19 20 21 22 23 24 25 26 27 28 29 30

No. NAME INSTRUCTOR

ADDRESS ZIP

1 2 3 4 5 6 7 8 9 10 11 12 13 14 15 16 17 18 19 20 21 22 23 24 25 26 27 28 29 30

No. NAME INSTRUCTOR

ADDRESS ZIP

1 2 3 4 5 6 7 8 9 10 11 12 13 14 15 16 17 18 19 20 21 22 23 24 25 26 27 28 29 30

No. NAME INSTRUCTOR

ADDRESS ZIP

1 2 3 4 5 6 7 8 9 10 11 12 13 14 15 16 17 18 19 20 21 22 23 24 25 26 27 28 29 30

APPENDIX P

COORDINATION OF *DISCOVERIES IN PROPHECY* VIDEOTAPES WITH *SEARCH FOR CERTAINTY* BIBLE LESSONS

Discoveries in Prophecy List of 26 sermons on video	***Search for Certainty*** Bible lesson number
1. LIVING BEYOND 2000	1
2. COUNTDOWN TO ETERNITY: WHY COMMUNISM FAILED	2
3. A WORLD IN TURMOIL	3
4. ANGEL 911: REVELATION'S ANGELIC CONFLICT	7
5. 2000 AND BEYOND: HOW TO FIND PERSONAL PEACE	5
6. ALIVE AT END TIMES: THE SECRET OF PERSONAL POWER	6
7. NEW AGE CONSPIRACY	4
8. THE BEGINNING OF THE END	9
9. FACING REVELATION'S JUDGMENT	10
10. WHY OUR STREETS HAVE BECOME UNSAFE	11
11. A 6,000 YEAR-OLD REMEDY FOR TENSION	12
12. THE GREATEST RELIGIOUS COVER-UP IN HISTORY	13
13. HOW TO IDENTIFY A CULT	14
14. THE COMING THOUSAND YEARS: THE GOLDEN AGE – OR WORLD DISASTER?	29
15. THE REAL TRUTH ABOUT NEAR-DEATH EXPERIENCES	16
16. HOW TO SUCCESSFULLY BURY THE PAST	18
17. WILL A LOVING GOD BURN SINNERS IN HELL FOREVER?	17
18. THE BIBLE'S ANCIENT HEALTH SECRETS REVEALED	15
19. WHY SO MANY DENOMINATIONS?	25
20. THE MYSTERY OF REVELATION'S BABYLON REVEALED	23
21. THE SEARCH FOR CERTAINTY	21
22. A FINANCIAL SECRET THE WORLD DOESN'T KNOW	19
23. THE MARK OF THE BEAST	26
24. THE UNITED STATES IN BIBLE PROPHECY	27
25. THE HOLY SPIRIT AND THE UNPARDONABLE SIN	24
26. REVELATION'S GLORIOUS CLIMAX	30

APPENDIX Q

COORDINATION OF *REVELATION OF HOPE* VIDEOTAPES WITH *SEARCH FOR CERTAINTY* BIBLE LESSONS

Revelation of Hope List of 27 sermons on video	***Search for Certainty*** Bible lesson number
1. REVELATION'S PREDICTIONS FOR THE NEW MILLENNIUM	1
2. REVELATION'S GREATEST END-TIME SIGNS	3
3. REVELATION'S BIGGEST SURPRISE	2
4. REVELATION'S STAR WARS – BATTLE BEHIND THE THRONE	7
5. REVELATION'S PEACEMAKER	5
6. REVELATION'S POWER LINE – SECRET OF A WHOLE NEW LIFE	6
7. REVELATION'S MOST AMAZING PROPHECY	8
8. REVELATION REVEALS HOW JESUS WILL COME	4
9. REVELATION PREDICTS THE TIME OF THE END	9
10. REVELATION'S ANSWER TO CRIME, LAWLESSNESS, TERRORISM	11
11. REVELATION'S ETERNAL SIGN	12
12. REVELATION EXPOSES HISTORY'S GREATEST HOAX	13
13. REVELATION UNMASKS THE CULT DECEPTION	14
14. REVELATION'S SEVEN LAST PLAGUES UNLEASHED	28
15. REVELATION REVEALS DEADLY DELUSIONS	16
16. REVELATION'S 1,000 YEARS OF PEACE	29
17. REVELATION'S LAKE OF FIRE	17
18. REVELATION'S WORLD OF TOMORROW	30
19. REVELATION'S NEW LIFE FOR A NEW MILLENNIUM	18
20. THE REVELATION LIFESTYLE	15
21. REVELATION'S FOUR HORSEMEN GALLOPING ACROSS THE SKY	*20
22. REVELATION'S LAST APPEAL	23
23. REVELATION'S MARK OF THE BEAST EXPOSED	26
24. REVELATION DESCRIBES THE UNITED STATES IN PROPHECY	27
25. REVELATION'S SPIRITUAL REVOLUTION FOR A NEW MILLENNIUM	21
26. REVELATION'S PROPHETIC MOVEMENT AT END-TIME	22
27. REVELATION REVEALS THE ULTIMATE ANSWER TO LIFE'S GREATEST PROBLEMS	25

The Search for Certainty Bible lesson titled, "Growing as a Christian" reveals insights on how you can draw close to God like the great heroes of faith in the past. It does not correlate specifically with the *Revelation of Hope* video.

**There are three additional lessons in the *Search for Certainty* set which will assist you in your growth with Christ. They are: "A Date with Destiny," "A Financial Secret," and "The Holy Spirit and the Unpardonable Sin."

APPENDIX R

COORDINATION OF *NEW BEGINNINGS* DVDS WITH *SEARCH FOR CERTAINTY* BIBLE LESSONS

New Beginnings List of 26 sermons on DVD	***Search for Certainty*** Bible lesson number
1. HOW TO KNOW THE FUTURE	2
2. SIGNS YOU CAN'T IGNORE	3
3. THE GREAT ESCAPE!	4
4. BY CHANCE OR DESIGN?	NONE
5. SECRETS OF ANCIENT SCROLLS	1
6. WHY SO MUCH SUFFERING?	7
7. ONE LIFE CHANGED THE WORLD	6
8. BORN TO LIVE FOREVER	5
9. FACING THE JUDGMENT WITH CONFIDENCE	9 & 10
10. WHAT HAPPENED TO RIGHT AND WRONG?	11
11. CREATED FOR SOMETHING BETTER	12
12. MILLIONS FOOLED BY A MYTH	13
13. TURN BACK THE CLOCK	15
14. WHAT HAPPENS WHEN YOU DIE?	16
15. EVIL IN CHAINS	29
16. WHEN THE SMOKE CLEARS	17
17. MAKING A NEW START	18
18. THE BATTLE FOR THE THRONE	NONE
19. THE GREAT PRETENDER	NONE
20. FOREVER MARKED	26
21. LET FREEDOM RING	27
22. SET FREE BY THE TRUTH	21 & 25
23. MESSAGES FROM BEYOND THE STARS	22
24. AN INVESTMENT YOU CAN'T LOSE	19
25. SURVIVING THE COMING TRIBULATION	28
26. THE BEST IS YET TO COME!	30

APPENDIX S

SAMPLE PRE-REGISTRATION FORM

FOR EVANGELISTIC MEETINGS (INSERT YOUR OWN LOCAL INFORMATION)

ADMIT ONE FAMILY

YOU ARE PERSONALLY INVITED TO THE

Revelation of HOPE

PROPHECY SEMINAR

Make plans to attend this thrilling multimedia experience.

GRAND OPENING PRESENTATION

"Thriving in the Tough Times Ahead"

FRIDAY, OCTOBER 4, AT 7:15 P.M.

FOREST LAKE ACADEMY AUDITORIUM
3909 E. SEMORAN BOULEVARD
APOPKA, FLORIDA

MAKE YOUR RESERVATION TODAY! CALL 000-0000.

FREE ADMISSION

TICKET REGISTRATION • RESERVED SEATS

NAME ____________________

ADDRESS ____________________

CITY ____________ STATE ______ ZIP ______

PHONE ( ) ____________________

EVANGELISTIC RESOURCES

2000
AND
BEYOND
MARK FINLEY

FINAL DAYS
MARK A. FINLEY

A HART RESEARCH CENTER PRODUCTION
Discover Jesus Seminar
With Mark Finley
GUARANTEED SECURITY IN AN UNCERTAIN WORLD

REVELATION'S
Predictions
FOR A
New
Millennium

NEW BEGINNINGS

DVD EVANGELISM

FROM IT IS WRITTEN

ONE DISC CAN MAKE A WORLD OF DIFFERENCE!

The *New Beginnings by His Word* Seminar is a cutting-edge, 26-topic evangelism tool developed by ASI and *It Is Written.* This powerful, yet easy-to-use DVD series combines the latest multimedia technology with 3D graphics to make Bible truths come alive. Preach it or play it—either way, this is your key to soul-winning success. *New Beginnings* is just one of *It Is Written's* many evangelistic resources. Please call **1-888-664-5573** today for a complete FREE catalog, or visit us online at www.iiw.org.

NOW AVAILABLE IN MAJOR WORLD LANGUAGES.

NOTES

NOTES

Materials and Additional Resources

Contact

Hart Research Center
P.O. Box 2377
Fallbrook, California 92088

Orders (800) 487-4278
Fax (760) 728-0879

Web address: www.hartresearch.org

E-mail: mail@hartresearch.org